Props On Her Sleeve

Props On Her Sleeve

The Wartime Letters of a Canadian Airwoman

Mary Hawkins Buch
- RCAF,W.D. (WOMEN'S DIVISION)

with Carolyn Gossage

DUNDURN PRESS
TORONTO • OXFORD

Editor: Carolyn Gossage/Derek Weiler
Printer: Transcontinental Printing Inc.

Canadian Cataloguing in Publication Data

Buch, Mary Hawkins
    Props on her sleeve: the wartime letters of a Canadian airwoman

ISBN 1-55002-294-6

1. Buch, Mary Hawkins – Correspondence. 2 World War, 1939-1945 – Personal narratives, Canadian. 3. Canada, Royal Canadian Air Force. Women's Division – Biography. I. Gossage, Carolyn, 1933-   . II. Title

D811.B82 1997   940.54'8171   C97-931822-X

1 2 3 4 5   01 00 99 98 97

THE CANADA COUNCIL | LE CONSEIL DES ARTS
FOR THE ARTS | DU CANADA
SINCE 1957 | DEPUIS 1957

We acknowledge the support of the **Canada Council for the Arts** for o publishing program. We also acknowledge the support of the **Ontario Arts Council** and the **Book Publishing Industry Development Progra** of the **Department of Canadian Heritage**.

Dundurn Press
8 Market Street
Suite 200
Toronto, Ontario, Canada
M5E 1M6

Dundurn Press
73 Lime Walk
Headington, Oxford
England
OX3 7AD

Dundurn Press
250 Sonwil Drive
Buffalo, NY
U.S.A. 14225

photo by Mark Lysco,
The Brockville Recorder & Times

Mary Buch was born in Montreal, and after World War II lived for many years in that city's Lakeshore community. She served on the local school board and was also actively involved in education at the provincial level. After graduation from College Marie-Victorin she went on to work in Youth Protection in Montreal.

In 1983, following her retirement to Brockville, she became immersed in genealogy and local history, and is a past-president of the Brockville and District Historical Society. Mary Buch has two sons and three grandchildren who live in the United States.

photo by Valerie Gossage Crook

Carolyn Gossage was born in Toronto and educated at St. Clement's School, the University of Toronto and La Sorbonne. As a teacher, her fascination with unrecorded history resulted in the publication of her first book, *A Question of Privilege: Canada's Independent Schools* (1977). This was followed in 1991 by *Greatcoats and Glamour Boots: Canadian Women at War and Double Duty* (1992), based on the wartime journals and sketchbooks of Canadian war artist Molly Lamb bobak.

A member of the Writers' Union of Canada since 1979, her time is divided between writing and research projects; but tutoring children on film sets - such as the Goosebumps series - adds a novel and entertaining dimension to her life. For recreation she maintains her long time love affair with the Great outdoors - sailing, skiing and bass fishing whenever and wherever possible.

CONTENTS

DEDICATION

for my granddaughters
Vanessa Buch and Katherine Buch
and for
Heather Strang
granddaughter
of
the late Marion Strang

ACKNOWLEDGEMENTS

First and foremost, the authors are indebted to the late Marion Strang, the recipient of these letters, for having kept them intact and in perfect order. Had she done otherwise, this particular record of wartime events and experiences would not exist.

Through their laborious efforts on the computerized transcription of the original letters, Mme. Mychelle Gay, a volunteer at the Canadian Museum of Civilization, and James Dawson of Ormstown, Quebec, both provided an incalculable contribution for which we extend our heartfelt thanks.

In addition, we are most grateful to Tim Dubé of the National Archives of Canada and the Canadian Aviation Historical Society, whose enthusiastic response to the collection when he first saw it in 1994, resulted in the Mary I. Buch Collection of letters, cards and other memorabilia becoming part of the permanent holdings of the Public Archives of Canada with unrestricted access. A thank you, also, to Jean Bruce for her long-standing interest in the preservation of these letters for future generations of Canadians.

Among those who generously offered their additional assistance and support in various capacities, we extend special thanks to Mr. Barry Barnes of Metheringham, Lincolnshire, U.K, Sgt. Margot (Norum) Beaulieu of Indian Head, Saskatchewan, S/L W. Bruce Brittain, D.F.C., of Ottawa, Sgt. Zella (Stade) Clark, Denman Island, B.C., F/L Tom Dailey and W.O. Duke Guilboard, M. Jean Houston, Toronto, Sara E. Johnson, Spruce Grove, Alberta, Mrs. John Mackenzie, Town of Mount Royal, Quebec, Miss Helen Neilson, M.B.E., of Hudson, Quebec, Mrs. Maureen Sampson, Brockville, Ontario, Mrs. Kenneth Strang, Victoria, B.C. and Mr. Gregory Weil, Senior Development Officer, Macdonald College, Ste. Anne de Bellevue, Quebec.

Mary Hawkins Buch, RCAF(W.D.),1943.

INTRODUCTION
by W. Bruce Brittain, D.F.C.

In the Fall of 1940, some 150 high school graduates descended on Macdonald College in Quebec to enroll in a one-year course that would qualify them as teachers and which – not coincidentally – in many cases would constitute their post-war employment insurance. It was here that Mary Buch's path and mine first crossed. Three years later they crossed once more on the RCAF Bomber Command base at Linton-on-Ouse in foggy Yorkshire, where I had arrived to pick up an aircraft. Then in early May 1945, just after VE Day, there was a chance meeting in London's Waterloo Station. Mary had just welcomed her husband, George, back from a German POW camp and I was on leave from hospital following my own POW tour.

It is now 1997 and once again our paths cross. Memories of the war years have begun to fade away, and for this reason I am grateful to Mary for making available to a wider audience – and especially to future generations – this account of one woman's wartime experience. This collection of letters not only splendidly documents an important facet of our social history but it serves, as well, to reaffirm the contribution of the many thousands of RCAF,WDs who enlisted in the service of their country.

Beyond the travails of Rosie the Riveter, today not a lot is known about the contribution of Canadian women during World War II, yet close to a million women were directly involved, replacing men in factories, offices, on farms and in a host of other traditionally male occupations. Fifty thousand of them were in uniform, and in the RCAF Women's Division alone, seven thousand served overseas, while another disappointed ten thousand persevered at home. In light of the fact that Canada's population then stood at approximately eleven million, these figures take on significance.

During my own introduction to flight training, the arrival of the first WDs at #6 Service Flying School was met with uncharacteristic silence. As student pilots, our focus and concerns were heavily slanted towards our own lot and the ever-present fear of being "washed out", but, inevitably, we questioned what life would be like for women in what had been, until then, a male domain, where Station life was no bed of roses for any of us. Would our life be improved or made more difficult by their presence ? Would they be able to carry their weight or would they be an added burden ? We also had concerns for them: these were girls who were our sisters, classmates and neighbours. How well would they tolerate the strict Station discipline and the occasionally rough male behavior? It must be remembered that this was 1942 and if a woman's place was no longer seen to be in the home, it certainly was not seen to be in the Armed Forces.

The answers to these questions were not long in coming. The novelty of sharing Station life with WDs very quickly settled into a routine, and in a sense, life seemed more normal than it had been before their arrival. Without anything being said, our dress, deportment and language underwent a miraculous improvement. The women were subject to the same discipline as the men; they neither sought nor were accorded any special treatment and demonstrated that they were at least as committed to their jobs. No one ever had cause to question their effort. They carried their share of the weight.

Once overseas, the women put up with the same conditions as the men – separation from family, wartime messing (mutton and Brussels sprouts), nonsensical orders and some incredibly bad living quarters. The low point was winter in a Nissen hut, an experience which few were spared. The utter cold and damp could be somewhat assuaged by feeding the hut's single pot-bellied stove with foraged scraps of wood or coal, as indicated in some of Mary's letters from Lincolnshire.

On Operations, the bond between all personnel was stronger than ever and the role of women more critical. Our very lives were dependent on the performance of women in a number of ways. Not the least of these was the care and packing of our parachutes. At 20,000 feet, a poorly packed parachute that wouldn't open when the rip cord was pulled had a bad impact. On bombing operations maintaining our link with home base, on whom we depended for vital information, was entrusted to the women who operated the wireless sets. Not infrequently, we looked to our Control Tower operator – usually a woman – as our savior; getting us on the ground in bad weather conditions and with aircraft from two squadrons all anxious to land in a hurry – some shot up, short of fuel, or with injured aboard and time running out. The calm efficiency of these women was a powerful influence in maintaining our "cool" in some rather "hairy" situations!

From an airman's point of view, quite apart from the historian's, the story of the part played by these women in wartime and by those in many other less visible trades should not go untold. These letters of Mary Buch, documenting her own experiences in her own inimitable style, have provided an important contribution towards this end.

Squadron Leader W. Bruce Brittain DFC
Director, The RCAF Prisoner of War Association
and Deputy Minister of Veterans Affairs 1975-1985

PREFACE

Most of the generation that went into uniform in World War II had been born either during or just after the Great War of 1914-1918. In fact, the 1920s and 1930s seem, now, to have been merely a lull between storms. By 1939, when Canada – like much of the Free World – was once more caught up in a war, we had just come through a decade of severe economic depression, made worse by the droughts in the Canadian West. Men by the thousands – many of them heads of families – were without work, riding the rails from town to town or hitching rides in freight cars in search of a job or, in fact, any kind of work that might generate a few dollars. Many a housewife responded to a knock at the kitchen door and a request for a meal. Whatever was available was doled out, and sometimes this included an overcoat or a pair of shoes.

For many young people, the possibility of going on to university had to be deterred, and more than a few left high school if they were able to find a job and contribute their earnings to the family income. Teachers, on the other hand, did their best to keep their students in school as long as possible, knowing that the job outlook was bleak and that every additional day spent increasing the knowledge and skill of their students was a day well spent.

Those of us who came of age during the late '30s and early '40s had lived our childhoods in the shadow of the First World War. Our parents' generation had been decimated and many of those who survived had endured unspeakable horrors. In my own family, my mother's brother had been killed in action while serving in the Royal Flying Corps in 1917, while her husband – my father – was wounded in the trenches of France during the final year of the Great War.

In 1939, with the onset of World War II, Canada's civilian population once again began finding ways of contributing to the War Effort. As the men enlisted, women all across the country took their places in factories and offices, on farms or as volunteer workers. By the war's end, over a million women had done their bit by replacing men who had enlisted in the Services and had helped provide needed goods, planes, ships and ammunition.

Rationing of food and fuel became the order of the day and since many items were in short supply, recycling was required as part of the War Effort.

National registration was made compulsory and a National Defence Tax was added to the regular income tax. The purchase of War Savings Bonds and Certificates became a matter of patriotic duty, and everywhere First Aid courses were filled to capacity.

From one end of the country to the other, the Women's Auxiliaries of churches, clubs and regiments knitted socks, scarves and mittens, rolled bandages and packed boxes and bales to be sent overseas to "the Boys". Local Service Clubs were established to provide hospitality for men stationed nearby or passing through on leave. Schools and businesses adopted members of staff who had joined up. The adage of "Make do, mend or do without" became an accepted part of everyday life.

Mail assumed major importance, both for those in the Services and on the Home Front. Hearts and homes were opened to men and women in the Forces who were far from their own families. Train services were greatly reduced for most civilians, who patiently accepted the fact that the troops must have priority.

But in June 1939, all this was still part of the unforeseeable future. Along with my classmates, I wrote my matriculation examinations at Montreal High School. By the following October, when the school graduation exercises were held, Canada had been at war for six or seven weeks, and already more than half of the 125 boys in that graduating class were in uniform.

I decided to stay on at Montreal High School for a pre-university year, and the following year enrolled in a teacher training course at Macdonald College in Ste. Anne de Bellevue, Quebec. Out of about 112 of us, only half a dozen or so were men, and on completion of the course, several of these immediately enlisted in the Armed Forces.

By late 1941, the RCAF had set up a Women's Division, and Frances (Graham) Blenkhorn, one of my closest friends, left her position as a dietitian at Macdonald College to enlist in the WDs as a Messing Officer. It all sounded very appealing, and I longed to follow her lead.

Then in the summer of 1942, while some of us were attending a summer course at Queen's University, a young female RCAF recruiting officer spoke very persuasively to a group of us about the newly-established Women's Division of the Air Force. At this point the Queen's campus was already thronging with handsome young men in uniform, who were combining their Officer training with the completion of medical school. These were exciting times for a girl to be young and single, with a perpetual stream of male visitors passing through town or stationed nearby. Impromptu get-togethers were generated at the drop of a hat, when someone's brother, or friend or cousin came home on Embarkation Leave.

Yet in spite of the good times, there was an almost frantic restlessness among those of us left behind. News of the fall of Hong Kong and the casualty lists from the Dieppe Raid had raised serious doubts about a swift end to the war. With the formation of the three Women's Services in Canada – the CWAC's (Canadian Women's Army Corps) and the RCAF Women's Division in mid-1941, and the Wrens (Women's Royal Canadian Naval Service) early in 1942 – many of us began to seriously consider our options.

By January 1943, I was halfway through my second year of teaching at Berthelet School in downtown Montreal and was sharing an apartment with another young teacher. My father had long since re-joined the Army and Chris, my older brother, was training to become an officer in the Black Watch – the Royal Highland Regiment of Canada. My younger brother, who was still in school, was with my mother in a small apartment. Since many of the younger nurses had gone on Active Service, my mother, having updated her qualifications as a nurse, was often on night duty.

The family was also still grieving the loss of my first cousin, Pat Hawkins, who had married a British civil servant posted in Burma. She had last been seen slipping off a life-raft in the Pacific, after the Japanese had torpedoed the ship

Lieut. Chris Hawkins, The Black Watch of Canada, R.H.R. (left) with his father, Major Stuart Hawkins, R.C.E. in late 1942.

Mary (Leggo) Hawkins, circa 1942, mother of Mary (Hawkins) Buch.

Marion (Gow) Strang, Dean of Women, Macdonald College, Ste. Anne de Bellevue, Quebec, 1936-1950.

she was on, which had been carrying women and children refugees from the war zone. Later her brother, who had enlisted in the RAF, was killed in a bombing raid over Germany. Canadian losses were taking a similar toll on hundreds of families all across the country, and my own personal malaise was growing stronger with each passing day.

My female colleagues at Berthelet hoped that if we did decide to enlist, our jobs would still be available on our return, since the men on Active Service had been given this assurance when they enlisted. On the other hand, because so many men had already left the classroom to enlist, was it patriotic for us to follow their lead? There were even rumours that teachers would be frozen in their jobs if the shortage became acute. Also, with my father and older brother both in uniform and on the move, what were my responsibilities toward my mother and younger brother? And then there was the apartment I was sharing. Would it be fair to break our agreement halfway through the year? It was all very complicated.

I decided that the time had come to seek the counsel of an impartial voice in the person of Marion Strang, a friend and mentor who was the Warden (Dean of Women) at Macdonald College. We arranged to meet for Sunday tea and I arrived out at the college with my mental list of pros and cons. Once I'd finished describing my dilemma, her response was spontaneously concise: "Go for it!"

The following day, immediately after school, I walked straight into the Air Force Recruiting Centre at the corner of Bishop and St. Catherine Street in Montreal. It was mid-January 1943.

After a brief interview, I was given an appointment for a medical examination and a further interview, and then sent home with forms to fill out. On my return I was also required to bring along letters of reference.

One of the people I approached for a reference was the Headmistress of Montreal High School, Catherine Mackenzie, known affectionately as "Auntie

Dot" and someone whom I considered a valued and respected friend. Whatever else she said in her letter of reference, she also raised the question of my physical stamina. Could I take the rigours of life in uniform? I had always been underweight – a skinny kid – and I later learned that her letter ended with these words of caution, "Take her at your peril."

As it turned out I passed the medical examination with no trouble, but the young Air Force physician was understandably concerned about the ninety pounds registered on the scales. Not much for a young woman measuring five-foot-six. So we struck a bargain. If I could return in two weeks with at least two more pounds to my credit, as the Medical Officer responsible he would assume that I was healthy enough to be accepted into the Air Force.

He also suggested that I'd be well advised to eat a hearty breakfast that included oatmeal porridge and to drink a good quantity of Stout every night before dinner. Then, just prior to reappearing for my medical, I was to avail myself of the drinking-fountain beside the elevator and to gulp down as much water as possible. This struck me as useful advice, but I pointed out that if I followed his instructions to the letter, his part of the bargain would be to see me promptly when I turned up fully primed with water. We shook hands and parted.

By the time two weeks had passed, I had managed to put on an impressive four pounds and almost before I knew it, I was IN! The Oath of Allegiance was administered in the presence of the Union Jack, and I was given the King's Shilling – a twenty-five cent piece indicating that I was now in the pay of His Majesty King George VI.

With orders to report to the Montreal train station at 1600 hours on February 19th and proceed from there to Ottawa for Basic Training at RCAF Rockcliffe, I had two scant weeks to settle my affairs and prepare for a whole new life. Although I am sure my parents both sensed my enthusiasm for the idea of joining the Air Force, I had not yet told them of my plans to enlist. With my father once again in uniform and my brother, Chris, slated for overseas duty, I suspect that my mother was slightly less than wholehearted in her congratulations, but she kept her own counsel. My father, for his part, was clearly proud and delighted to hear my news, and the blessing I received from his quarter was unreserved.

When I told Chris, who was already an officer-in-training in the Army, that I was off to join the WDs, he puffed on his pipe before imparting his brotherly words of wisdom. "I s'pose I don't need to remind you that crossed legs, like crossed arms, are the best form of defence."

In the two short weeks after my enlistment, there were many things to be attended to, including the termination of my teaching contract at Berthelet and the storage of my belongings. Hélène L'Espèrance, with whom I'd been sharing an apartment, was gracious about this sudden turn of events and subsequently decided to join the Women's Army Corps. In fact, of a group of six of us who had been together at Queen's the previous summer upgrading our teaching qualifications, four had enlisted before the year was out – two into the Air Force, one into the Navy and Hélène into the Army. Dorothy Raguin, a former school friend and colleague at Berthelet School, left teaching shortly after I did and enlisted in the Wrens. And so it went.

During the hectic course of these final weeks of civilian life, my sister-in-law and I travelled to Trois Rivières for my brother Chris's graduation from his officer training course. It was here that I first met the man I would later marry. George Buch, one of my brother's fellow-officers, was also in the Black Watch. Later, on post-graduation leave, he arrived in Montreal. It happened to be the eve of my departure for Basic Training at Rockcliffe when he turned up at my door. As the larder was bare, we tramped the streets in an unsuccessful foray for beer before returning to the now-dismantled apartment to settle for toast and tea. Our paths would not cross again for several months, when we both found ourselves stationed in Halifax, Nova Scotia.

Over the next three years, in addition to George, my parents, and my brother, I exchanged letters with a number of other family members and friends. Since wartime mail delivery was irregular at best, people who wrote to each other frequently took to numbering their letters to establish a semblance of sequential order. My mother, for example, knew that if letters #17 and # 20 arrived, the two missing epistles would turn up sooner or later to fill in the unexplained gaps.

One of my regular correspondents was Marion Strang of Macdonald College, who had given me the nudge of encouragement that led me to enlist in the Air Force. Aside from the respect and admiration I held for her, there was an additional motivation for me to send as many letters as possible in her direction. Her son, Lieutenant Kenneth Strang, had been with the Royal Rifles of Quebec in Hong Kong in December of 1941, and once he became a Japanese prisoner of war there was virtually no communication in either direction.

In the European theatre, the Geneva Convention regarding P.O.W.s was operative and, with a great deal of assistance on the part of the International Red Cross, lists of those taken prisoner were made available. For the most part letters and parcels to prisoners got delivered and on occasion severely wounded or chronically ill prisoners were exchanged. In the case of Japan, however, no such agreement had been signed; nor was surrender an accepted element of Japanese ideology – all of which precluded reciprocity. As a result, when Hong Kong fell, there was no notification of who was alive, wounded or dead, and virtually no one escaped to bring back first-hand reports. Finally, months later, word came through that Kenneth Strang was alive, and his mother received one brief card from him but nothing more. In late 1945 he was liberated, in moderately good condition, although anyone who endured what those prisoners had been subjected to was inevitably affected for life.

In the interval, I felt that my own letters describing the joys and vicissitudes of life in the RCAF Women's Division might at least provide Kenneth's mother with a minor diversion while she waited.

At the time of writing I had no idea that each of these WD letters of mine was being kept in tidy sequence and would be given back to me by Mrs. Strang after the war was over. Had I been aware that all these letters had been carefully set aside for my return, I might have written more self-consciously, but as it was, I simply wrote about whatever was happening or was on my mind at the time. While much of the content of these letters is subjective, it reflects the gamut of day-to-day experiences in the Air Force – initially here in Canada and later in England. In retrospect, some of the recorded ups and downs seem trivial, but with the passage of time, other elements have taken on greater significance.

Marion Strang lived for another quarter of a century after

Lieut. Kenneth Strang, The Royal Rifles Of Canada, Quebec. P.O.W. Hong Kong 1941-45.

the end of World War II and was close to eighty when she died in 1972. She never asked me to use her first name, nor would it have occurred to me to suggest otherwise. This says more about the difference in our generations than it does about the warmth and duration of our friendship. There were certain proprieties to be observed and maintained. It was as simple as that.

In re-reading this correspondence, which has lain untouched for half a century, I now see a pattern in the posting of our group of WDs, which certainly made little, if any, sense at the time, but which now takes on a shape of its own as a small part of a much larger plan. These letters, interspersed with observations from the present, relate events and experiences of times long past – as fragmented bits and pieces of shared joys and common sorrows.

PART ONE
Taking the King's Shilling
February–April 1943

Those responsible for setting up the three Women's Services in World War II had responded to the need to provide female replacements for men sent overseas on Active Service. It was agreed that these Servicewomen would be subject to the same kind of discipline, rules and regulations that governed their male counterparts and would be moved about within Canada and Newfoundland – and later in Britain, whenever it was deemed necessary to do so. An essential beginning to life in the Service was a period of integration known as Basic Training and these initial letters to Marion Strang are an indication of the sense of belonging that we all experienced right from "Day One".

#7 Manning Depot
Rockcliffe, Ont.
Sunday, Feb. 21, 1943

I've been sitting looking at the triangle above, thinking that "the spirit is willing", even if the mind and body are about to lie down and cross their feet!

Last week is just a golden haze in my memory. Most of it was spent dashing hither and yon from early morning to late at night. I do remember that I didn't have a single meal other than breakfast at the apartment, and that one night, I didn't come home to bed – stayed at Seymour Avenue. *(This was the home of Auntie Dot – the Headmistress of Montreal High School, which I had attended since the fifth grade.)* There were two parties Wednesday and Thursday – and Thursday I took time off to see *In Which We Serve.* (Don't see it if you don't want your heart broken. It is extremely powerful.)

Thursday, George Buch came back from New York and came over for what was left of the evening. Friday, *(February 19, 1943)* the train left Windsor at four, with nine of us headed for Rockcliffe.

William Brittain, Principal of Macdonald College of McGill University.

The train was crowded; the usual week-enders, plus a crowd of airmen. I came up with Col. Brittain *(William Brittain, the Principal of Macdonald College of McGill University, was appointed an Honorary Lieut.Colonel in the Canadian Army when the Canadian Women's Army Corps took over part of the College campus at St. Anne de Bellevue early in 1942. For the rest of the War, Col. Brittain had to try to oversee a College, keep McGill happy, and act as a go-between whenever the Army and the Faculty met head-on. Those who knew Dean Brittain were aware that he would have preferred research and teaching to administration and was not especially at ease in his role as an Army officer. On occasion he would carry his cap rather than wear it, in order to avoid the need to return salutes.)* I think he was half-amused, half-amazed. I kept mislaying the Official Documents which had been given into my safe-keeping for the trip. We had dinner in the diner, but I was mighty hungry by the time we all reached here, about nine-thirty.

A plate of beans (our first) kept body and soul together a little longer, and there was much to do before we could crawl between the sheets. (There *are* sheets, by the way!)

Came morning, and the beginning of the job. Mechanics' exams – all about the weight of the feathers on a hen, as well as other tests – spelling and addition and all sorts of things. We signed papers and more papers, got our Leave passes, waited for a medical exam, etc. etc. At six p.m. we had a Flight Meeting, were introduced to our officers and non-commissioned officers and received our first instructions.

There are about two hundred and eighty in our Squadron, which is divided into four Flights. It's the largest Squad of recruits they've had yet, and I think the Sergeant is having quite a headache over it.

The Barracks are in the form of an "H", with a corridor down the centre of each upright part of the "H". The rooms on either side of the corridor hold about twenty double-decker beds, so there is no lack of company. I sleep in an upper. They are warmer than the lower ones, but rather precarious for the first few nights!

Saturday night I had a late pass, and went in to Ottawa to our cousins' for a few hours. The buses which used to run on this route all got burned in the garage ten days ago, so taxis are in order.

This morning we had our first Parade – Church of England – at ten-thirty, and Communion afterwards. This afternoon we went for our kit, but have not a complete one yet. My feet are too big and my neck is too small, so I'll have to wait awhile for a few things.

The food is remarkably good. There must be about seven hundred served at each meal in the Mess – cafeteria-style. All time now is measured by the proximity to the next meal, and we find no trouble in packing food away.

There is no Wet Canteen on the Station, and all beverage rooms are out of bounds for us while we are taking our Basic Training. We have passes from five to ten p.m. every day...from noon until twelve-thirty on Saturday, and from noon until ten Sunday. So far we have been busy, and I think we will continue to be so for the rest of the Course. If we are lucky, we get a 36-hour pass at the end of four weeks. Otherwise we must wait for a "48", the first week after we begin our new course.

The officers, sergeants and corporals are all magnificent, and I think we are going to enjoy our work.

We have classes from eight-thirty to five, though the day begins at six-thirty in the morning. I am on Snow Duty tomorrow, so I'm praying for fine weather – without a flake!

We are a conglomerate crowd from all over the Dominion. I have been hearing of the advantages of the West – the broad, clean streets of Winnipeg, and so forth. There are a very few pansies who have been grousing about the food, and there are two or three noisy people in our barrack-block, but the others are shaking down pretty well. The adjustments necessary to be made are terrific, and it will take some time to shape into good soldiers, but we have hopes... I have already distinguished myself by pouring milk from the Corporals' table, but have not yet tripped any officers, which is something! (*Never* underestimate the respect due to a Corporal!)

There is to be a movie tonight starring Errol Flynn so I think I'll go over to see it. There is plenty to do in Recreation Time, though no privacy whatever. I can nap at odd times, with all the noise, and I foresee no trouble with insomnia!

We have the usual amount of scrubbing to do and every third day will see me on Orderly Room or some other duty. No fires to watch – yet! And P.T. doesn't begin until next week.

We have had no time to be homesick, nor are we likely to have. I miss a few things in "Army life" – bath-tubs, for one thing! You just can't sleep in a shower, no matter how you try. I have not found any extraordinarily congenial friends with the same interests as my own, but that will come with time, I think.

One of the officers who was at the Recruiting Centre in Montreal, Assistant Section Officer Da Costa, has been posted here, which was a pleasant surprise for us. It's amazing what one familiar face will do for a person!

RCAF
No. 7 Manning Depot
Rockcliffe, Ont.
Feb. 23, 1943.

Still flying, but with one broken wing and no propeller. I don't remember many times when I've been too tired to dance; but this is one of them.

Yesterday, after the usual routine of Parade, Roll-call, Inspection and so on, we went through Equipment and finished – as far as possible – our kitting. I still have no overshoes and my feet are still wet. No rubbers, no shirts with small collars, but I have my hat, trench coat, shoes and stockings, tunics, skirts, ties, and polishing kit, as well as the dunnage bag. We have been issued with the old-type uniform, which makes me happy. We may get a new hat and tunic later in the Spring.

In the afternoon I had an interview with the Selection Board, and I have been assigned to Clerk Operational. This means that I stay on at Rockcliffe Station, across the way, for perhaps four weeks and then get posted to an Air Station on one of the coasts. It will be rather hush-hush, and I shall not be allowed to take any written notes at lectures but must memorize all I see and hear in the Tower. It should prove interesting work. Wish I knew a bit more about it. They won't tell us anything until we get to the course. Our instructors will include two WAAFs from the other side. At the moment I can scarcely tell a fighter from a bomber. I'd be a great comfort to the enemy!

It was imperative that all of us be inoculated against communicable diseases, so everyone received three injections, a week apart, against typhoid fever, paratyphoid A and B and tetanus (known as TABTS). Injections against diphtheria and whooping cough were routinely combined and administered on three separate occasions. There was also a test for scarlet fever, followed by five injections if needed. Re-vaccination against small-pox was routine. It was an accepted fact that on Basic Training, needles were nothing more than an inescapable part of the package.

Late yesterday afternoon two hundred of us had five needles apiece. So that is over for a few days. Many of the girls passed out – from sheer nerves, I think. Three fainted in bed this morning. I wish you could have seen us trying to climb into our top bunks last night. It was too hopelessly funny. We all helped each other, and the last one had to make it herself, with the rest of us cheering each time she almost made it, and booing when she fell back.

I feel all right except for the beating I take each time we have to line up for anything. Our parade was a pretty sick affair today, with stiff arms jutting out in all directions. This morning I got finger-printed, and this afternoon the dentist took me on. That was about all we needed to make our happiness complete – a dentist. We had our teeth checked for future reference...

We have to stay in our lecture room long hours, and get shifted off to various buildings for interviews and tests. This involves a great deal of waiting, and so we write during that time. Once the initiation is over, we shall have lectures regularly. In the meantime we are on our feet a great part of the time, and we get awfully sick of *people*.

I was invited to Ottawa friends' for dinner Thursday, but it will have to be postponed for a day or two. We are Confined to Barracks on Thursday night to scrub the place. More fun! It is no great hardship, as we all get together with pails, and more water than we can use, and mop and mop.

Today we all made our Wills. We were rather in the mood, I'd say. It's about time to turn in. Morning comes early when one has to rise and shine.

No. 7 Manning Depot,
Rockliffe, Ont.
Feb. 26th, 1943

This Station has more than its share of humour... A camera would be in order in the mornings, when we climb gracefully down backwards from our bunks, but cameras on the Station are forbidden, lest the Enemy derive comfort. The poor Enemy is apparently not to have the benefit of even a snap of the WDs.

We aren't allowed to wear any of our uniform until next week, when we shall have had pretty sound instruction on saluting and general behaviour.

At Rockcliffe, where we were assigned for our introduction to life in the Air Force, Warrant Officer Wright was responsible for giving us instructions in the fine art of marching and drill. He was a great bear of a man with red hair and a moustache. Introducing raw recruits to the basics of drill is an unenviable task at the best of times, yet he demonstrated a high degree of patience with his charges. His charades of a woman walking in high heels or pulling down her girdle on parade became memorable examples of how not to perform as part of a marching unit.

The injections are over for three weeks, thank heavens. I am still immune to scarlet fever, diphtheria and small-pox, but must have two more typhoid – tetanus needles. TABTs are the worst, so we shall be glad when they are over. I had a very bad reaction by Wednesday evening, after two hours of drill and P.T., and no one will ever be able to convince me that the fact that I have already had injections for typhoid in civvy street within the last eight months had nothing to do with it. However, I'd have to be dead or unconscious before they'd get me on Sick Parade and no one has ever died of pain yet, so here we are – very happy in the Service and entirely satisfied with "Canada's War Effort".

Yesterday I was on Barrack Fatigue, as perhaps I told you. Up at 6:30, as usual, had a shower and a hearty breakfast, and was back in Barracks by seven-twenty. Made my bed in four seconds flat, tidied the locker which I share with the girl beneath me, and was ready for Fatigues. We have very tricky overalls (Teddy Bear suits) which we don for our heavy work.

Out came the pails and brooms and dusters. The beds have to be looked over, the windows opened, the blinds straightened, the floor swept, the beds and suitcases and window-sills dusted, the ash-trays emptied, the towels and kit-bags straightened, the blankets and pillows set right, and the garbage disposed of. I arrived at lectures at eight-ten (ten minutes early) and joy, oh bliss, ours was the best Barrack-block on the Depot...

Had lectures, parade, drill, P.T. until five, and then supper. From then on we had to prepare for the C.O.'s inspection, which took place today. The C.O. inspects every Friday, and she brings her little dog with her. The dog doesn't look like a blood-hound, but he can smell food anywhere, in spite of the odours of disinfectant and soap. He leads her right away to any cache. He spat grape-seeds on the floor this morning. Not mine, but they could easily have been. We aren't supposed to have any food in the barracks, and secretly we think Mr. Jones (the dog) is meant for efficiency rather than ornament.

I have been spending my spare time on my buttons. Matches, Brasso and elbow-grease work wonders... but slowly! I am determined that they shall be as well-kept as Dad's, but there is lots to live up to if that is to be so....

> *The first Saturday afternoon that we were allowed into Ottawa from Basic Training, a group of us made a bee-line for Birks' with our tunics to have the buttons buffed. New brass buttons have a sort of protective lacquer on them which can normally be removed by using Brasso and plenty of elbow grease. Our idea was that Birks' buffing machines could do the job equally well and save us a great deal of time and effort. There was an added benefit to all of this. Since the Air Force buttons bore the albatross insignia, it was widely known that after repeated polishings, the feathers gradually got worn down and this served as an indication of lengthy service. When we trooped out of Birks', the buttons on our tunics had definitely lost all traces of their tell-tale feathers and we looked as if we'd been in uniform forever.*

Our flight lectures are most interesting. We had an address from a Flight-Sergeant yesterday on the care of the hair – styles and treatment thereof. Another lecture was on "Etiquette and Bearing". A third, on fire-fighting and the use of implements, how to act, and when. Still another was on the equivalent ranks of the Army, Air Force and Navy. Others have been on how to wear the uniform, how to care for it, and so on. The Padre spoke today on Morals and Religion, Life, Liberty and the Pursuit of Happiness, etc..

Some of our lectures are given by NCO's, others by Officers. Every one of the lecturers knows her stuff, and they are all cracker-jacks.

I cannot say too much on the subject of our officers. Their efficiency is remarkable, and the wheels turn so smoothly that the co-operation between NCO's and Officers, and the speed with which they accomplish their duties, tempered with the cheerfulness of them all, can produce nothing short of a happy and efficient Service. They have been selected for their qualities, and the Powers That Be were not asleep at the switch when they gleaned these gems. It makes even a humble recruit feel that nothing short of the best will do.

The Station is a beautiful one. One would think that Barracks would detract from a landscape, but not so. White buildings, green window-frames and red roofs make for attractiveness. We were on a march yesterday, and we enjoyed the scenery – while sidestepping puddles. We don't miss a sunrise or a sunset, and the afterglow is always a source of joy. Walking across the Station from the Canteen to the Barracks on a starry night with Taps sounding out, is something I shall never forget.

Our meals are continuing to be excellent; so it was no first-moment enthusiasm which overcame me at the beginning. For lunch today we had cream of carrot soup, roast beef, potatoes, turnips, celery, cole slaw, apple pie, tea or milk and all the bread, butter, jam, we wanted. There is always cheese on the table and no one goes hungry unless by choice. The R.C.'s can have fish on Fridays if they want it. With an undisclosed number (running into four figures) eating in the Mess, I call it remarkable that the food is so well-presented.

There is an excellent library here. I am reading a book of Aldous Huxley's just now – *Point Counterpoint*. There are all the large newspapers in the Canteen, and some magazines.

We are off tomorrow at noon, and I hope to go to my cousins' for the rest of the day. I'm to be on twenty-four-hour call the next day, so Sunday will hardly be a "Day of Rest". But I'm so much in my element. We all are. We just love it. There are only two things I want – starting with a bath-tub. And the other thing takes a bit of explaining. When I get home, I'm going to line everyone up for meals, and then I'm going to be at the head of the line – just once!

By the time we made our next trip to Ottawa, following our earlier excursion to Birks', we were all in uniform and saluting everyone in sight. In the nation's capital there was certainly no shortage of uniformed personnel, so we got plenty of practice. I even recall some discussion among ourselves about saluting the doorman at the Chateau Laurier, since his hat was resplendent with gold braid.

No. 7 "Manless" Depot
March 5th, 1943

The rookies are learning to march on ice – both feet off the ground, skidding around corners, falling flat on the word "Halt". Great fun!

If I shuttle back and forth from one subject to another, it's probably because that's the way life is these days.

Kit Inspection is tomorrow, and we must have every blessed article marked with name, rank, number and date of issue. My bed-fellow and I share a locker, and it is simply crammed with a conglomeration of civilian and military clothing. We hope to be sending some of our stuff home soon. Until then it is a trifle difficult to approach the standard of neatness required.

Drill, P.T. and Flight Instruction are taking up nearly all our time, and the days go by like greased lightning. P.T. looks after those lazy muscles in a way that nothing else could. I have played Basketball a couple of times in the evening with some of that so-called excess energy that is ours at the end of the day. Drill is great fun and we all look forward to it. Doing things in unison is a thrill all by itself and at this rate we must all be three inches taller.

The esprit de corps of the Squadron is really shaping up now and cooperation is not just a word. The Squadron Concert comes off on Tuesday. We had our first rehearsal tonight.

Hair is proving quite a problem. I've had mine thinned considerably, so I cannot now be accused of being either a "Wispy" or a "Fuzz-Buzz" – both major offences. But I look a trifle ridiculous with my mop in its present state. A severe roll is indicated, but just try to get a brush-cut to play ball. No can do.

My greatcoat all but swallows me up. It's very warm, but after a couple of hours of tight buttons at my neck, I'm ready for a jar of cold cream on the outside, and any kind of lubrication on the inside (water preferred, of course!). We are to be issued with the new hats before we graduate and they will be our walking-out hats from then on.

Basic Training included deportment, the correct way to wear the uniform and a thorough knowledge of what was referred to as the "King's Regulations". These included an umbrella phrase that covered everything not already specified as forbidden or compulsory and read "...Anything contrary to good Air Force discipline." This might include any possible misdemeanour, from sneaking in late to leaving a sloppily-made bed.

An identification bracelet, a watch and a signet-type ring were the only adornments permitted and make-up had to be inconspicuous. We were allowed to wear civilian clothes for specific occasions, and then only with written confirmation from the Commanding Officer. Woe betide the servicewoman whom the Service Police recognized in unauthorized civilian dress.

It occurred to some of us on Basic Training that perhaps we could get away with wearing unironed shirts under our tunics – providing the collars were pressed and neat. We had forgotten, of course, that our officers and NCOs had all been through Basic Training themselves and that they were well aware from their own experience that the idea of wearing an unironed shirt was far from original.

Someone in our midst decided to give it a whirl. After Parade, the officer in charge said to her NCO, "Would you kindly ask that airwoman to remove her tunic?" And it soon became abundantly clear that the offending party had failed to adhere to the regulations. I am not certain whether she was sent straight to the gallows or settled for life imprisonment. In any case, punitive measures were taken and none of us contemplated taking shortcuts when it came to ironing our shirts while on Basic Training.

Did I say that I thought I was about through with injections? Only ten more to go. I'd gladly give my right arm for Victory. I've only myself to thank that I have to give it, and the left as well – for injections! I feel like a blinking pin-cushion. I can't even bear the sight of a sewing needle now. Think I'll get a plug put in one arm, pull out the plug and shove in the stuff. It might save some time.

The onion-peeling and snow-shovelling and floor-scrubbing go on as usual. Montreal won't have any post-war snow-removal problem if they enlist us women to do the job – we're whizzes with a pick by now. It's wonderful (?) what two weeks will do for people!

Rockliffe, Ont.
March 10th, 1943

There is a bad epidemic of influenza rampant, and wouldn't you know I'd have to be right on the spot at the time. So here I am, plunked in the Station Hospital, and probably here for a coon's age. What would you say if I told you that I had been plastered for four days? The mustard kind, and pretty hot stuff!

There are a number of us together from our Squadron. Our chief worry is that we won't graduate with the others next week, but it can't be helped.

Perhaps when I'm better I'll be able to give you the inside dope on a Station Hospital. "Views from a White Bed", or "Four Walls and a Ceiling", or something equally exciting. I know you'll be fascinated!

This isn't exactly the way I had planned to spend my Coming of Age, but Toujours Gai, and Vive le Sport and so on.

There was a shortage of overshoes in snowy Rockcliffe in February 1943, and this may well have contributed to an outbreak of throat and chest infections that laid many of us low. I landed in a room in the Sick Quarters with Mona (Langley) Murdock, a young airwoman from my squadron, who was suffering from strept throat. I had been diagnosed as having bronchitis, yet I was instructed to gargle, while Mona inhaled Friar's Balsam for her non-existent respiratory problems. Someone had obviously prescribed for each of us the treatment for the other's ailment and at the time it struck us both as pretty hilarious. It also marked the beginning of a friendship that we were able to maintain after we were both given identical postings. Less than a year later, Mona was my matron-of-honour when George Buch and I were married in London, England.

It was during this same session in Sick Quarters with Mona that I learned about Orderly Officers. We already knew that when the Officer of the Day appeared at a meal and asked if there were any complaints, it was definitely intended as a rhetorical question. In the Station hospital, a pleasant young WD officer with her sergeant and corporal in tow proceeded to ask the patients if there was anything we'd like. I don't recall Mona requesting anything, but I commented that I'd appreciate having some stationery. The officer turned to her sergeant and said, " See to it that this airwoman gets some stationery" ; whereupon the sergeant turned to the corporal, who was busy taking notes, and repeated the order.

After about a quarter of an hour, the corporal reappeared with the notepaper and launched into a lengthy diatribe about protocol and how no one should ever make a request to an Orderly Officer under any circumstances. We noted the near-felony and governed ourselves accordingly.

St. Patrick's Day
March 17, 1943

A very bruised and battered AW2 [*Airwoman Second Class*] is looking forward to a trip home starting Friday. The weather has been just as deplorable here as I imagine it was elsewhere. We have marched in cold, sleet, rain, mush, slipperiness and what-have-you. Route marches, rehearsals for the big Graduation Parade tomorrow, three more injections, extra drill. A weary life, altogether.

But comes yet the week-end! That's all that keeps us going. I hope to stop off at Ste. Anne's on Sunday afternoon.

Our exam was not too hard and I think I passed. One less worry for us now. The Squadron pulls out tomorrow night. Nine of us stay on for our course, which starts Monday.

As we were about to complete our stint as airwomen-in-training, one of our female administration officers reminded us of our responsibility to uphold the good reputation of the RCAF Women's Division, " Remember to watch your language, girls! You never know when there might be gentlemen present..." In fact, during the entire course of my years in uniform, the majority of us seldom used or heard coarse language, substituting RCAF or RAF slang expressions for obscenities.

When they entered the Women's Division, a few girls already knew which Trade group they'd be assigned to. Some had been dietitians in peacetime, so automatically they became Messing Officers in the Air Force. Others had had experience in transport or as dental assistants; but the majority of us had to undergo testing while on Basic Training to determine which Trade we'd be best suited for. Nine of us were selected from our Squadron to remain at Rockcliffe for another four weeks to take the Clerk Ops course... sometimes lightly referred to as " Clerk Oops".

We knew next to nothing about what would be expected of us, and anyone who did told us nothing. All we knew was that we were strictly forbidden to bring any paper or books into our classes; nor were we permitted to take anything out with us. Whatever we learned had to be learned on the spot.

Our instruction was given by four RAF non-commissioned officers who had been through the Battle of Britain. Initially they had been sent out from England to escort the first class of WD Clerk Ops to New York, where they'd learned the necessary codes and devices for work on this side of the Atlantic. From New York, these same British NCO's proceeded to Rockcliffe to give the Clerk Ops course there in a so-called temporary building. (I have since lived long enough to know that there is nothing quite as permanent as something designated as temporary; so the building may well still be there.)

We marched down to the Ops hut from the Manning Depot on the first day of the course and took our places. It was late March and the sun was starting to work its magic on the remains of the snow. Small patches of brown earth were beginning to appear in the area beside the building, revealing several stakes with markers on them, where someone had attempted to plant a Victory Garden the previous summer. As we sat in rapt attention, our instructor walked over to the window, " See those markers out there?" We all nodded in the affirmative. "Those mark the graves of the WDs who have failed this course..." So began our introduction to the world of Clerk Ops and, not unexpectedly, we were an attentive lot.

Rockcliffe, Ont.
March 23rd, 1943
2100 hrs.

We have completed two days of our course. It is strenuous work, but interesting. We are still entirely at sea in the Operations Room, and we wonder if we ever will learn enough to be of any use. But there is the feeling that one is close to action – or might be – on a Station. There is definitely not a chance of our getting overseas and we were asked what the next choice of destination was. I asked to be sent West. It will depend entirely on how the strength is in the two coastal commands, whether or not that crazy dream comes true!

It seems just as strange to be back here after two days' Leave, as it did to be back at home after five weeks. The passing of time always mystifies me – it's an unknown and unpredictable quantity.

RCAF (W.D.) Route March, Parliament Hill, Ottawa, April 1943.

Sunday, April 4th, 1943

This has really been a day of leisure for us. We slept in until eight-thirty this morning, had breakfast at nine, did our odd jobs and went to Church Parade at a quarter to ten. We had an hour off before dinner, and the afternoon has passed slowly and pleasantly.

I am only now getting around to some of the details I should have attended to weeks ago. At last, I have marked my blankets and today I got around to putting buttons on a couple of shirts. Our next two weeks promise to be frantically busy ones, so we are starting to pack some of the things we know we shan't be needing. I know what will happen...Some well-meaning NCO will ask to see my summer issue or I'll discover the day before we pull out that the baggage tags are at the bottom of my dunnage bag. It happens every time.

The Route March yesterday was a big thrill for us. We were taken to town in beautiful Air Force buses and formed up on Parliament Hill. The Precision Squad was first and then the Clerk Ops' Flight and, after us, the Technical Training Wing, composed of girls who had either been specially selected or who had qualified on the Parade-ground.

We gave an "Eyes Left" as we passed the War Memorial and then we went up Sparks Street, along Bank, down Laurier Avenue and back to the Hill via Nicholas and Rideau Street. I thought surely my hat would blow off into the Canal as we went over the Laurier Avenue Bridge, but it didn't ... miraculously.

It was a gorgeous Spring day and the route was lined with people (most of them colonels and upwards – there *aren't* any civilians here). It seemed so right, somehow, to be swinging along in the sunshine, and the Band was wonderful. There was no effort at all to stepping out, and I shall not soon forget the feeling I had.

I had another letter from one of the girls who has been posted to the Wireless School on Queen Mary Road. They don't seem very happy, and it makes us realize that the luxury and the friendship of the Manning Depot are things to be treasured. Funny, isn't it, how lonely one can be in the heart of a large city? Here the fellowship is indeed "something to write home about", and we couldn't be more comfortable (unless we had inner spring mattresses!).

I want to dispel any illusions about the type of person one meets and works and eats with in the Women's Division. I'm sure it's true of the Army and the Navy as well. The girls are bricks – right through.

The work is going well. It would be easy to get panic-stricken and my feet are often very cold when I stop to think about it. But there is no time for thought and while we're working we must be "on the qui vive" every moment.

Our major task as Clerk Ops would be to plot in-coming and out-going aircraft; receiving information over our headsets about their identity – friendly or hostile – their whereabouts, direction, height and so forth. In addition we were expected to be well-versed in aircraft recognition, be able to do a bit of dead-reckoning and some meteorological calculations. We also received a few demonstrations of Radar devices, some of which we'd be required to use on the job. By the end of April half of our class was posted to the Eastern Air Command in Halifax and the remaining half was shipped off to the West Coast.

Friends celebrating in Hull, P.Q. following graduation from W.D. Clerk Ops training in Ottawa, March 1943.

Collection of M. Jean Houston

Friday p.m.
April 9, 1943

Life is good. The results of our exam were worth celebrating so Wednesday night a few of us came in to town and had dinner (plus beer) at the Chateau Grill. When we returned to Barracks I shined all the shoes in our wing. The girls think they might buy me more than one bottle next time, and perhaps I'd do their buttons as well!

The unofficial posting list has come out via the grape-vine. It looks like the East for me. My closest friends are going down to Halifax, so I am thrilled about it. I should be content either East or West, but now that it is pretty certain, I'm looking forward to the Maritimes. I don't think I need to tell you that we should see and hear lots that is exciting down there.

We get posted again from Halifax in a few weeks, so I am on the lookout for a quiet spot in Newfoundland or Labrador. One never knows.

So far I have successfully concealed from the Fighter Control School the fact that I speak French. They want (I hear) a number of bilingual Clerk Ops for the Gaspé district. Can you picture a cosy winter at a certain summer resort – me and the wolves? Patriotism is not enough ...!

There was a poem in circulation at the time which more or less sums up what so many of us were feeling as a result of having accepted the King's Shilling ...

Anticipation
(or Dreams of a WD)

Oh for the morn, will it ever be born,
When my bed is not hastily made,
When without any rush I can eat up my mush,
And not have to dash for parade.

Oh for the hour when physical power
I need no longer summon each night
To spring to an upper, so late after supper,
Before I can tuck me in tight.

Oh for the day when for two-thirds the pay
That a man gets for just the same job,
No longer in line must I stand to get mine,
Just one of an organized mob.

Oh for the time – let me say it in rhyme -
When I'll live in undisciplined bliss,
When I'm able to say each hour of the day
The Service Was Never Like This!

Flt. Officer Frances Douglas

PART TWO

Eastern Air Command, Halifax, N.S.
April – July 1943

Operations Room
Eastern Air Command,
April 22, 1943

Here we are – not quite established, but camping in temporary quarters for the time being, and reasonably comfortable.

It certainly was wonderful to get back to civilization last week-end. Four days of luxury is as good as an eternity at the time, and the realization was every bit as good as the dream!

Paddy Seccombe came down from Toronto on the night train Tuesday and had breakfast with us at Auntie Dot's. We left for Bonaventure Station at 11:00 a.m. and got down there only to find that we couldn't go until seven-thirty in the evening. It was rather an anti-climax to have fifteen airwomen and sundry civilians gather for a final farewell, only to disperse for another eight hours. We were able to phone Auntie Dot not to come down, so her time was saved, but the whole performance was awfully silly – and typically military, I thought. It was particularly hard on the girls from Toronto, who had left a whole day earlier to be in Montreal at the appointed hour.

We finally did shove off at seven o'clock that evening. Auntie Dot and Pauline Turner and Grandfather Hawkins and Miss Wright, of Montreal High School, came down to the station to see that we really did go this time.

There are no complaints about the way the CNR treats the WDs. The train was filled with Air Force boys and the Airwomen were given the drawing-rooms. We had a wonderful time. The porter made up our berths for us early, and by 9:30 we were settled with chocolates and some books. We went to sleep about 10:30 and didn't waken until we reached Campbellton -practically the first call for dinner!

The boys were awfully good to us. We played at Bridge in the afternoon and spent the entire second evening entertaining each other reading poetry aloud. It was one in the morning before we got out here and had a meal. I don't

Miss Catherine I. Mackenzie ("Auntie Dot") Lady Principal, The High School for Girls, Montreal, Quebec, circa 1942.

remember going to bed, but I was there when they wakened us at six this morning, so I must have turned in at some time or other.

In Halifax we Clerk Ops lived at the "Y" Depot, which was the last stop for Air Force personnel on their way overseas. Each day we were transported to the Command Control Room by truck. Halifax was overcrowded with sailors and airmen, and we were warned not to travel on our own – especially after dark in the blackout. Not that any of us would have dreamed of it.

We went to town by truck this morning from the "Y" Depot, where we are housed in Nissen huts [*tunnel-shaped huts made of corrugated iron with cement floors*]and had our breakfast after we got there. There were a lot of details to adjust. We begin work at six tomorrow night, so we are free until then. We work in shifts, night and day, alternately, with a "36" every four days.

We are allowed to live in the city if we prefer. That's a joke. Nice work if one could get a room – not even a decent room -just a room. The accounts of this place were grossly understated, believe me. I have not the slightest intention of walking around alone in broad daylight, much less after dark. The Five Wise Virgins would need to trim their lamps here... Anyway it would be too expensive to live out, even with our subsistence allowance, and we'd miss all the fun of the Station, so we are resigned to travelling in by bus or truck – a matter of five minutes' ride.

The Recreation Centre here at the "Y" Depot is the best equipped in Canada, they say, with bowling, tennis, billiards and all the rest, right on the Station. Movies every night, dances twice a week, and three million lonely men. Rather a grim prospect in some ways. Wouldn't you know it, just as I get sent down here, George Buch goes away for a six weeks' course. He may be back before I leave. We are to be here for an indefinite time, so who knows?

We lack the comfort and (semi) privacy of our other Barracks. They are larger, less scrubbed, hotter and colder by turns. The food leaves something to be desired, but we are very lucky to have all we do. No complaints.

I had a telegram first thing this morning from Sybil Dennis at the Wireless School, wishing us all luck and I sent one to Mother to say we had arrived. The Censor crossed out "toujours gai". Evidently that quality is an offence when down here! Some of my letters will likely be opened ...

The phrase "toujours gai!" taken from Don Marquis's book Archie & Mehitabel *was very much in vogue at the time and one can only assume that the censor in question suspected a secret code. Most people communicated by letter and the postal service was generally fast and reliable; however, occasionally a telegram was in order. Long-distance telephone calls were still considered a needless luxury and were reserved for urgent messages. Telegrams and cables often bore news of an emergency or worse. The contents of many wires were telephoned to their recipients providing they had a telephone. If the telegram contained bad news of someone near and dear, who had been reported missing, wounded or dead, boys on bicycles rode around town delivering tragedy in the form of a yellow envelope.*

Wartime censorship was such that a cable might easily be overtaken by a letter, which was cheaper and often faster as well. Another form of censorship was delay; if the contents of a cable contained any information that might be useful to the Enemy, the lapse of time would render the information useless. References to one's location or unit were definitely taboo; as was information about troop movements, individual or group destinations and even discussion of the weather. Despite these precautions, people in the Services quickly learned ways to circumvent the censors by referring to a particular landmark or local point of interest.

Operations,
Eastern Air Command,
April 26th, 1943

The middle of the night is not exactly the time I would choose to write letters, but it is nearly four a.m. and things are quiet. We have thirty-six hours off when eight o'clock finally rolls around, and we're getting tired so we can sleep...

Easter Day was perfectly heavenly here. We came off the night shift and went right to Church Parade at ten. The Service was held out on the Square in the sunshine. The boys were lined up full strength and we WDs had a place in the shade beside the Band facing the square. We were on a little knoll, so we had an excellent view of everything.

So impressive was the Service itself that I wept all through the first Easter hymn. Martial music is moving anyway and the boys looked so fine.

Settling down has been a matter of busy happiness. I suppose Maritimers get used to the prevalence of fog, just as natives of Saskatchewan grow up to ignore gophers, and Torontonians swell with pride and perceive no ridicule on hearing their city called "The Good". A growing fondness for pea soup and molasses almost convinces me, without undue alarm, that occasionally I shall be taken for a Quebecer, but that does not matter.

A sudden excess of cigarette lighters is replacing the homely match in my life. Dad gave me his Ronson when I was home. He had two and this one was a presentation from his Company when they went Overseas. I took it reluctantly and bought a cheap one here to substitute, intending to return Dad's to him. Today a parcel arrived from my uncle, containing two lighters, a tin of fluid and a box of wicks.

There was a four-page, closely-typed letter accompanying, giving explicit instructions about the working of these little Swiss toys. After prodigious effort, in which sines and tangents flew freely and lay shattered in heaps on the floor, I found three ways of operating the spiral dingus. It's not a job to be entrusted to anyone of sudden temper or bibulous habits.

Mother gave me two flashlights – one a pocket edition, the other an average size, so I shall be well lit, one way or another!

We spent Saturday over at Dartmouth getting acquainted with things there. A beautiful trip over and back, and one I thoroughly enjoyed.

I am busy procuring warm things against a colder climate [*Newfoundland*] and we may be away before the Queen's Birthday. Rumours are rampant. One can't depend on a word one hears. I should consider it a miracle if it happened, knowing that a humble AW2's chances are slight, but one can always dream.

I am dreading unpacking my dunnage bag. The top layer was damp upon arrival and there is no place to spread things out and air them, so I keep postponing the evil day. It is nearly six now, and there have been interruptions here and there. Another two hours and we can scoot out for breakfast. Happy thought!

Operations, E.A.C
May 6th, 1943.

The sparks have stopped flying from the wheel, for a while at least. The lull after the storm – and a pen close at hand…

Sunday was our first opportunity to visit a church in the city. Paddy Seccombe and I – along with two of the boys – went to St. Matthias' Anglican Church and to dinner at the Nova Scotian afterward. You probably know that that is the CNR Hotel here. We had by far the best meal that it has been our privilege to stand in line for since coming here.

The axe fell today. After we came off the Graveyard Shift and had had our breakfast, we were sent to a Medical Parade. The M.O. told me gently and cheerfully that I was to begin having injections. I expostulated, to no good purpose. Had I any record of any previous injections? No? Neither had the

Office. Your left arm, please... So I had my fifth TABT, and it was chalked up as my second. I was recovering from my fourth and extra one when I saw you last.

Altogether I have now had sixteen needles and it looks as though there are fourteen more in store for me. I see now why people desert. If you don't hear from me for a while, tune in to Jim Hunter and hear how an AW2 died in Dartmouth Hospital from an overdose of Paratyphoid...

We shall be staying here for some time to come, according to the latest rumours. It's a prospect which excites me not at all. The cost of – not living, but existing – in this city is rather serious. But there it is – and here we are!

It's nearly midnight, and we shall be off soon. Bed sounds good after having been up since six-thirty yesterday morning. A Kitting Parade yesterday and that unspeakably horrid M.O. today have robbed us of our few hours' sleep while we were off duty and we are just a little fagged.

Operations, E.A.C.
May 7th, 1943

I never feel like asking anyone to write, but when letters do come it's the most wonderful thing. The picture has changed again. It may be another false alarm. One never knows.

Was out on the most wonderful party last night, after counting on a "36" to recuperate from the last mad week. It was cancelled and I went to work at eight this morning – with overnight bags under my eyes. My shattered nerves!

I'll be an AW1 [*Airwoman First Class*] in another week. I'd like to be able to say that it is the result of Gallantry and Meritorious Service in the Field, but I'm afraid it is just one of those things which, like an automatic right dressing or the accustoming of oneself to a hard bed, simply comes to you after three months in the Air Force.

Halifax homes were very hospitable and the women who organized and ran the ANA [Army, Navy and Air Force] Club for Servicewoman were exceptional in every sense of the word. Not only did they provide a drop-in centre where we could meet friends, have coffee and some home-cooked food, they also entertained myriads of us and "the Boys" in their own homes and for many of us this made Halifax a very warm and agreeable place.

Our social calendars became extremely full as there were men from all three services continually coming and going. As well, I had linked up again with George Buch, my brother's Black Watch friend and fellow officer, who was now in the Halifax area. We attended many regimental functions and went picnicking on the northeast Arm a few times. Talk of marriage eventually came to the fore, but we agreed that, since George was due to go overseas within a couple of months, it would be best to wait it out for the time being.

Ops – E.A.C.
May 11th, 1943

Am in the very pink of condition, having just had about twenty hours of nothing but sleep and then four meals in the space of almost as many hours. I have been curled up on the sofa at Army, Navy and Air Force House, wondering about the weather way down yonder. Paddy and I are stepping out in a few minutes.

Airwoman Mary (Hawkins) Buch on day off in Halifax. Summer of 1943.

I had dinner and spent the evening with the Whitfords here Friday. They are friends of friends in Montreal and most kind. They promised not to put themselves out too much and I hope they didn't, but they certainly know how to "entertain the Troops" so to speak – and besides, never was there such chocolate cake!

Saturday night Paddy and I went to the dance at the Nova Scotian with two Sergeant-Pilots from Toronto, and had a wonderful time.

Sunday evening four of the girls and I went to the Vesper Service at St. Paul's Church. It fairly drips with Canadian history. I had visions of Indians and fur traders and little fishing boats all the time I should have been engulfed in silent prayer. The building is quaint and they tell me it was the first Anglican cathedral outside the Motherland – 1750 or so. I hope to go back during the week some time to look around a bit.

Yesterday was our day off. Happy occasion! I got up in time to spend a few hours visiting friends and came back to ANA in time for a practice blackout.

May 14th, 1943

The kind of day when I feel like taking a long walk – and work begins at four p.m., so I can't. Our shifts are all mixed up again. I think we're getting "fried" somewhere along the line, but we were allowed to sleep in this morning, so perhaps I'd better not say anything!

I have been spending the day drying out blankets and belongings. The atmosphere has been – to say the least – penetrating of late, and our Barracks have been very damp.

Poor old Paddy has been on charge, and is Confined to Barracks with restricted privileges and extra duty for seven days. She made a remark in a letter home which was quite innocent, but it happened to hit a couple of nails smack on the head, and the Censor caught up with her. She has to report to the Service Police at the guard-house every hour, so we don't see much of each other these days.

A tri-service snapshot taken at the Army, Navy, Air Force Club, Halifax, N.S. 1943. Mary Hawkins Buch, RCAF, W.D. on the right.

I've made such a habit of falling asleep here at the ANA Club that Mrs. Jones, one of the kind ladies, has taken pity on me. She keeps referring to me as "That Poor Child" and has asked me several times to go home to their place to bed. It always happens that I am just on my way to work, but she has been kind enough to ask me to stay with her the next time I have a "36", which I look forward to doing.

Spring is just arriving here and things are beginning to turn green.
Pay Parade calls and is not to be ignored.

When we enlisted early in 1943, the basic pay for women was two-thirds that of the men: ninety cents a day as against $1.20. By mid-1944, Trades Pay for servicewomen had been made equal to that of the men, although the basic rate remained unchanged.

May 24th, 1943

We have been working frightfully hard and our shift is short-staffed, which means eight hours without a let-up and we rather resemble the proverbial wet rag when we come out into the bright world again. Another group is expected to join us shortly and it will make a great difference.

Life is still gay around here. Saturday afternoon, I just chanced to run into a boy from home – Bill Weber, who got married a couple of weeks ago and immediately got posted down here on a course. He's a Lieutenant in the RCA and doesn't know a *soul* here, so we were like two long-lost friends. We went to a movie and then to the ANA to talk about our friends. I was mighty glad to see him and enjoyed the evening with him.

Our medical documents arrived today – too little and too late! Saturday's job (injection) worked its evil worst today, so the M.O. let me spend the afternoon in the Barracks. I felt fine by seven o'clock, so went to dinner with Montreal friends at the Nova Scotian.

I received a letter from Hélène L'Espèrance today which she had addressed to me on the ninth of March! It went overseas accidentally (I wish I could!) and was returned this week. Rather fun to read about a week-end of skiing, in May!

I think I should trot off to bed now. Six a.m. comes pretty quickly and it's nearly eleven now. We are eating at another Mess while ours is being painted, and the food is a great improvement there. No dogs and cats wandering at large, which I rather like, considering that I have seen the dogs sample the soup in our own Mess before we do!

E.A.C.
May 27th, 1943

I've just fought an uphill battle on behalf of the French-Canadians. My Air Force friends don't seem to think they're worth saving and I stand alone in their defence. Rather futile, considering I'm hopelessly out-numbered, but it makes an interesting subject for fireside discussion...

Ye Olde Grave-Yarde
Shifte,
May 31st, 1943
(very early)

This damnable climate! I dream of the fond days when I had dry blankets and wonder if they will come again. To top it off there was a flood in the Ablutions today and we've been trotting around in rubber boots, trying not to laugh too loudly in case we awaken the sleepers.

Finally got around this week to the tailor and now my uniforms look more nearly as though they were meant for me. We are wondering whether we will get the new summer uniform – or whether we will need it if we do get it ...

Measles are rampant in our Barracks and people look so funny when they get up in the morning – all red in the face. It is leaving us shorter than ever on the shift, but we are managing. The ranks are depleting and Dartmouth Hospital is filling up. A good chance for a holiday, I'd say. I must look into it.

Dorothy Raguin and I met at the ANA Club yesterday. She looks fit and is getting a kick out of the Wrens. She was in the School for Teachers the year before I was and was teaching at Berthelet. She left a month after I did – to join the Navy. I asked her if the Wrens get their tot of rum and she said, "No, but apart from that everything is just the way Nelson left it". I know what she means.

I tried to phone home tonight. Sat around for a couple of hours in a hotel lobby, while Halifax attempted to get a line through to Montreal. Spoke first in French and then in English and then in French again. Finally got through. A blackout added to the complications... Think I'll carry some barbed wire with me – to discourage lonely sailors in the dark.

I spent the evening with Paddy. We have not seen each other to talk to for ever so long. Like greeting a long-lost friend, since our spare time so seldom coincides now.

On Sunday Mrs. Jones (ANA Club) asked me if I'd try to get a pass to sleep out all this week. I explained that it was Graveyard week, but she said she didn't mind having a tired A.W. stagger in at nine in the morning to retire to a room to sleep most of the day. So ever since, I have been there. I come off this shift at eight tomorrow and I'm to go to Mrs. Jones' for the day and come back to work at four P.M. We work evenings all the coming week.

Last night was my night off, so I slept nearly all day yesterday and all night as well – with time off to go to Halifax's only bowling alley and just about dislocate my arm, since I have not bowled at all, lately.

The Jones family has been simply wonderful and I've enjoyed it all so much. They are darling people, and we are taken right in as members of the family.

This afternoon I took seven-year old Peter Jones to the Fair. I don't know when I've had such a kick out of anything. We went on all the rides and he held on for dear life – and wanted more. He is a very good youngster and it's a treat to have him around.

Have been out every night this week for dinner one place or another with friends. Is it any wonder that I think the residents hospitable? Kit Watson has sailed and George Buch has gone on leave now that his course is finished, so the gaiety will subside a bit. [*Kit later went down with his ship.*]

Letters this week from my pals in Newfoundland. They have seen a few icebergs, aeroplanes and ducks; have good quarters and lots of recreation. All the places the officers frequent are Out of Bounds to the ranks, which is breaking a lot of hearts where fiancées are concerned. Altogether, though, it sounds very favorable.

My brother, Chris, is home from what he calls Niagara-*in* the-Lake, and has gone to Farnham again. He gets his furlough at the end of the month.

Guess I told you I'm reading *Barometer Rising*. The Halifax setting is aptly described.

We are not to be allowed to try our next trade test until the Fall. September probably. Meantime we are learning a lot in other lines. Nothing that will help us much in our own work, I suppose, but at least we are learning and that's something. So it will be months before I am an LAW – Leading Airwoman. Think I'll write a book on the care and feeding of pigeons in the interval.

We were issued our new purses today – very swish blue imitation leather and the strap makes me feel as though I were wearing a Sam Brown. We don't wear them on one shoulder, as the Army girls do, because we have no epaulet.

They promise the new summer Walking Out uniform soon. The Precision Squad marched in it yesterday, and it was a Good Show. Rather like Old Home Week for those of us who were training at the same time as the Squad at Rockcliffe. This is my last night on the four to midnight shift for a while. To morrow is my day off and I go back to work Friday from eight to four. I am to stay with the Jones' tonight and tomorrow. Mrs. Jones has asked me to go with them next Friday to their summer home at the western tip of Nova Scotia. It will be a short week-end for me, but I'm looking forward to even twenty- four hours there. The blossoms should still be out and it sounds wonderful.

Tomorrow, if the weather permits, we are going to picnic out on the Arm. There are some very lovely spots close by and I have been spending this week trying to camouflage a deathly pallor, with rather peculiar results – all the left side of me burned to a crisp and the rest uncooked as yet.

Paddy is going over to Dartmouth for two months or so – just after we had found a beautiful double room out near the Arm. I shall be able to see her on our nights off, which is about as often as we have seen each other lately anyway.

Paddy and I were checked for smoking in Barracks after Lights Out last night. We got in from work at one a.m. and the Sergeant was making her rounds. I nearly caused a fire trying to put the silly cigarette out. I don't know what the consequences will be, but they won't be serious – I hope!

Long lazy Hawkins in a canoe —!

The dentist has been taking up my mornings. I finally got around to going to a civilian, having tried to see the Army dentist ever since February. This chap is a dandy and inspires confidence, which is rather a good thing, considering I shall be seeing a lot of him.

Now that a noted Briton has returned home safely, I may tell you that two of us had the honour to invigilate during part of his travels. It was a thrill at the time. [* *During the latter part of May 1943, Churchill had meetings with President Roosevelt in Washington. The meetings were given the code-name "Trident" and the return flight to England was routed over Eastern Canada.*]

Isn't it too bad about Leslie Howard? [* *The actor, best known in North America for his role as Ashley Wilkes in* Gone With the Wind, *was shot down on a flight over the Bay of Biscay on June 1, 1943.*]

Things are going very well. Life continues to be in technicolour in Halifax. Whom the gods love slip on a banana peel. I am wondering just how long this will last. Were it not for the ties in what here is called Upper Canada, I doubt if I should ever want to leave Halifax. (I can say that on a day like today!)

The chief topic of conversation is, of course, the old one of postings. When, where, why, for how long? It adds a spice of delightful uncertainty to life, and one always wonders whether one's next meal will be in Gander Bay or at Sydney, N.S.

This Watch is about over and I must look as though I have been working, so I shall start now to putter about for the next half hour.

Meatless Tuesday,
(not to be confused with
Chooseless Meat Day)
June 15th, 1943

When we get calls from the Lower part of the River, we always have to add three hours for Greenwich Mean Time and subtract one hour from our time to catch on to the idea of where the sun is at the other points. It was tricky at first, but I am quite used to it now. Everything with us runs on GMT, of course. "1700hrs. G.M.T." etc.

This is the week of eight to four p.m. daily. Getting up in the morning and going to bed at night, just like ordinary mortals.

I had a day off last Thursday and spent it as though there were nothing in the world but leisure and fun. Went to the Jones' after work at midnight Wednesday, slept until noon Thursday, loafed in the garden until about three. At four several of us WDs went out in canoes on the Arm and had a simply superb time just paddling about. We had supper at the North West Arm Rowing Club and then I played tennis until dusk.

About nine o'clock I went back to the Jones' place to put in some transplants for Mrs. Jones. She is going to wonder just what sort of graduates an

Agricultural College like Macdonald produces! I know I put the tomatoes in the right place, but am looking forward to watching the petunias appear among the melons ...

Saturday night I went to the Station Dance with a Pilot Officer from Toronto. Sunday, Paddy and I had tea at the Jones' with all the family and three P/O's [*Pilot Officers*]from the "Y" Depot, who are transients. Last night I got rash and laundered everything I own. Tonight I think I shall tumble into bed at a reasonable hour.

Paddy has gone to Dartmouth on temporary duty for two months. She can get back over here on the Duty Boat after working hours, but it is a most unsatisfactory arrangement all around and I hate it. Paddy will like Dartmouth after the first week. It's always the first week anywhere that's the hardest, but just now she's pretty blue, so I have to be cheerful for both of us.

Friday night Graveyard begins again for me. I come off work at eight Saturday and shall try to catch the eight-ten train to Annapolis to the Jones'. Pat Moore, a girl who came up here from the B.W.I. to enlist, is going down too, and we are to drive back on Monday with the Jones family, in time to go to work at midnight Monday. It sounds so wonderful to have three whole days! Thirty-six hours is the longest I've had off since we started this business. It nearly broke the Sergeant's heart to give me the time, but actually it simply amounts to taking my days off for this week and next consecutively. It probably sounds silly to you that I should wax so eloquent about a week-end, but if people only knew what hot water and dry blankets and the prospect of some sunshine meant! All that apart from the fun we have with the Jones' youngsters.

Shortly after we came to this Outpost of Empire I got very run down – stopped, in fact. I passed right out at work one day. The first time in my long life. The M.O. decided that Iron was the solution, and since then I have been just roller-skating around. The fact that I stopped having injections about that time had nothing to do with it, according to the M.O. So we must attribute all the glory to the Iron tablets. The M.O. is always right, you know...

We lost one of our friends in a very nasty episode. Fortunately the man involved was caught, so there is one less nut on the loose...You see what I mean, now, about the lamps being kept trimmed? It could happen anywhere. Halifax is not exceptional; but all the same, we are being careful to travel in dozens.

Several of us have joined the North West Arm Rowing Club. Swimming in the Arm is out of bounds for us until they consider the water safe, but there are other advantages and Service folk get a very reasonable rate. It's a lovely spot, very similar to the lakes of northern Ontario and Quebec, but the water is salt of course.

I heard a rumour that Lloyd's of London was accepting bets that the war would be over this summer. I think they must mean *next* July, though things are certainly cheering up and I'd wager Italy will be ours by the Fall. That's as far as my prophecy goes.

George Buch returned yesterday, and I hope to see him tomorrow night. He was in Montreal all week, so I shall be learning about the bright lights of the big city, no doubt.

My friend Pat Moore's uncle (Lieut. Commander P.F. de Freitas) came ashore and provided some gin the other night at dinner, so I had a Collins. Daily Routine Orders announced yesterday that the Liquor line-ups are out of bounds for all WD personnel, and the boys are not letting us forget it! Not that there is anything in the Arid Desert of Nova Scotia to line up for; nor that I would necessarily run all the way down to the Liquor Control if there were. (Sour grapes, you see, must be our only substitute for the Juice of the Grape.)

It looks as though it will be September before I land home. Leave is due on the nineteenth of August or after, but we are so short of people that it may well be later on in the autumn. One can always dream, though. I want to fly up if I can. The difficulty lies in the fact that if I go to any of those remote spots outside Canada, I am closed in for six months at the very least, and likely longer. However, there will come a day ... And in the meantime, we are entirely happy where we are.

Halifax, N.S.
Wednesday, June 23, 1943

An influx of mail today brought me two uninformative post cards and some all-day suckers.

It's hard to believe that the last week of June is upon us. The longest day of the year has come and gone. I don't know where the time goes. This week we are working during the day, so the long summer evenings are ours to while away.

Some new girls arrived last week, praise be. And now – guess what ? We are to have seventy-two hours off every week ... work six days and have three off. It is pretty wonderful! We are having four shifts, three working and one off each twenty four hours, so there will be lots of time to do all the things we've been planning to do all along.

The tail end of last week was pretty hectic. I worked all day and all night Thursday, with just enough time off in the evening to have dinner with George and go for a walk. We arrived at the Rowing Club in time for the dance which was on, but I had to be back at H.Q. by midnight. Friday I worked in the afternoon, stayed at the Blue Triangle that night and caught the early train to Granville on Saturday.

Thanks to Mr. Jones, I had one of the few parlour car seats going down and I spent the entire five hours out on the observation platform, drinking in the scenery. The Jones family met me en masse at the Station and although I had already had a meal with some Wren friends on the train, I tucked away another lunch with them at the house. We lay out in the sun for part of the afternoon and then drove over to have a look at Deepbrook. Saturday night we went to a dance at a neighbour's. Mrs. Jones had invited some Navy Cadets from Deepbrook to come over – about forty of them. We had a very good time, though I missed Pat Moore, who was to have come with me from Halifax. She had to work, at the last minute.

Sunday we drove to Kedgemakooge and went to Church in the evening. Monday we loafed in the sun and started homeward about four o'clock. The drive up the Annapolis Valley is quite beyond description. It's not very often words fail me!

The sleep, sunshine and five meals a day have made their mark and I look very much like a tough old beet just now. (Not the tender little young beet, but the hard red variety.) It was a pretty marvelous three days, altogether, and I enjoyed it.

George Buch was to have been on deck tonight, but he has to be Orderly Officer for the next three days, so it's no go. However, we are to go to the Black Watch dance at the Mess Saturday, which is very exciting. Civilian clothes are indicated, since I cannot appear among the exalted like this (and I do mean like this!) My little blue job with all the brass buttons is not just the thing. It will be quite a thrill to be in civvies again – disguised, as it were.

Sunday we hope to go on a picnic at some spot as yet unknown. I suppose the weatherman will have his say, but I hope it's fine.

With the new long Leave between shifts, there is now some chance of my getting home, if I can persuade someone to work one of my shifts for me. However, I am not counting on it. Ninety-six hours would give me two days and a night in Montreal, but twenty-seven hours each way on the train somewhat offsets the pleasure of such an expedition. Besides, one doesn't dare look ahead three weeks. Newfoundland is too close! George won't be here very long, though he is in the same position of not knowing when. There is one thing about the prospect of Newfy. At least there would be no doubt about where I was to be for the next eight months. Once there, one is settled for a while.

I feel tonight as though I were writing from a different world. Mrs. Miniver expressed it aptly when she said that the centre and the axis of the universe are always where the person happens to be ... Montreal, Halifax or Vancouver. I can see you raising one eyebrow. You've never heard Halifax described as the hub of the universe before, have you?

Halifax, N.S.
June 28, 1943

Saturday night we went to the long-awaited Opening of the Black Watch Mess. There was a dinner first and the Band piped us in, which was a thrill. The dance began at ten and went on far into the night. I met several of the lads who had been at the Graduation in February at Three Rivers, class-mates of Chris' and George's. It was a strange feeling, at first, to be in an Officers' mess after so long. My feet kept coming to attention in an annoying way and it was all I could do to keep from saying "Ma'am" to the C.W.A.C. Officers – even my contemporaries! My disguise as a civilian didn't keep up very long, since a couple of the boys remembered that Chris's sister was in the Air Force. However, we had a wonderful time – needless to say.

I am staying at the Blue Triangle Club while on a seventy-two. Tomorrow I go on the four to midnight shift. George is to be away all week in bivouac, but comes next Saturday...

We moved downstairs to a new Operations Room this week and while it is beautifully outfitted, the cockroaches in the basement have not been trained and we are having quite a picnic. We hope in time to have them beaten down into good messengers. In the meantime they are behaving badly. The new Room, like the other, of course has no windows. The officers finally broke down on Friday and allowed us to remove our coats, which was a relief. A starched collar is rather useless and not at all decorative in weather such as this. And still no sign of a summer issue. I am wearing the same amount of clothing that I did at Rockcliffe against the chill winds off the plains.

I had to come down to earth sufficiently to keep a dentist appointment today. It looks as though one of my two best wisdom teeth is going to have to come out, which the dentist says will mean taking some time off, since the stupid tooth is not entirely through yet. I had an X-ray this morning and shall know more in two weeks when I go back. The Air Force is going to like this!

At this point, the possibility of a posting to Newfoundland came up, however since I had, by this time, become the object of George Buch's undivided attention, my desire to exchange Halifax for a remote posting had diminished accordingly.

July 30, 1943

Last night I was sent for and offered the posting to Newfy which, in May, I would have leapt at. I shook my head. The Flight Sergeant laughed and winked, so I stay here a while longer, at least. I look back at my disappointment of two months ago, when most of the others pulled out of here and I was packed for a whole week – living with one toothbrush and some pyjamas rolled up, ready to hop a 'plane – and then got left in the end.

However, I have a reprieve for a time and the Flight Sergeant was rather wonderful, I think, to even bother asking me. So many would just have sent someone, and dat would have been dat.

Three of us have taken a very nice room on South Park, not far from Eastern Air Command, the Jones' and A.N.A. The other two girls are Pat

Moore (B.W.I) and Helen Woodcroft. We move in tomorrow or Saturday, and I can hardly wait. Some day I shall describe the Depot Barracks to you, and you will understand then why even a blanket on the floor in a quiet corner would be an improvement. As it is, our room has furniture, a huge cupboard and two very comfortable beds – a double and a single. All the essentials.

The landlady draws the line at drunken brawls, but apart from that, there are no limitations. Just as at Queen's, one is requested to "Shut the Door" when one comes in, which is a reasonable request, I think! There have been shift-workers living here before, so presumably the lady of the house is resigned to odd hours by this time.

The "Daily Rumour Order" has it that within the next month we shall all have to live in Barracks. But even a month of hot water, privacy, freedom, what-have-you, sounds like bliss and it will be worth it.

Yesterday I received a parcel from the A.P.W.T. – otherwise known as the Association of Protestant Women Teachers. The parcel contained some Air Force notepaper, soap, cold cream, four Air Force linen handkerchiefs, bobbie pins and Kleenex – all very useful – and the latter two unheard-of down here. I was quite touched that they should have thought of it. Wasn't it good of them?

We have a new WD Officer, who has just come back from England. She had lots to tell us about our sisters in the WAAF and all that goes on in the work there. One can always learn and we have accumulated a lot just from odd chats with her.

It's just about midnight and we shall be changing the guard shortly, so I had better finish up and pull myself together. An unbuckled tunic is not "the thing"!

PART THREE

Operations Training – RCAF Sea Plane Base,
Dartmouth, N.S.
July – November 1943

*After spending several months in the Control Room at Eastern Air
Command, Halifax, a group of us was posted to the Sea Plane Base across
the basin at Dartmouth in July 1943. Six of us were selected for further
training in Operations. One of our future duties would be to "scramble"
aircraft, which meant calling the Hut so that one or more Flights (two
aircraft apiece) – could be sent up as a defence against potential enemy
aircraft, known as "bandits".*

*So we learned the instructions, " Scramble, Red Flight" or " Scramble,
Blue Flight ", knowing full well that, at that time, there were too few
planes available for purposes of defence. Had there been a land or an air-
attack on the East Coast, we would have been woefully unprepared. The
sentries and guards for the most part had no ammunition. The reality was
that Canada was contributing men and planes where they were considered*

to be needed most — and that meant overseas. Meanwhile the Cansos and their crews were searching for the U-boats that had been menacing the Gulf of St. Lawrence and the waters off Newfoundland and the Atlantic provinces. For our part, we on the ground ploughed ahead, learning the routines that would be used either at some other Station closer to the action, or — God forbid — right there if things got hot.

At this juncture I had been in the Air Force almost six months and was itching to get an overseas posting; but they were few and far between and for the time being Newfoundland appeared to be the closest I would get to the war. In the interval we made the most of our time in Dartmouth.

Operations RCAF,
Sea Plane Base,,
Dartmouth, N.S.
Fri. Aug. 13 (!), 1943

This may not be just the best day to start a letter to anyone, but since I'm back on Ye Olde Graveyarde Shifte, I don't think much can happen before morning and I'll mail it right away quickly before the Gremlins of Friday the 13th get hold of the letter and mix up the address — or whatever Gremlins *do* on the 13th.

You know by now — if my card from Moncton reached you — that I passed! How or why, goodness knows — I don't. I didn't expect to. I got a recommendation as well, but that's neither here nor there, since there is no room on OTC (Officer Training) for weeks and weeks and no room here for officers — yet. The solution is obvious. You can keep an A.W.1 at work after she has been trained and she will be roped in for any job that is handy. Not so an officer. There have to be specific duties laid down for the latter. So here we are!

The trip to Moncton was a stroke of luck, combined with the good management of the Chief, who has been simply wonderful about giving me time off since the course ended. He practically said I didn't need to return from Halifax until after George had to go back.

I met The Ocean Limited in Moncton as scheduled and we had from five till midnight on the train together. Wednesday morning we rushed about like mad, checking George's baggage and doing a hundred and one messages. He left in the afternoon and I whipped back to the Station to work. My forty-eight wasn't quite up, but it seemed the only fair thing to do, in view of the Controller's kindness.

There is a chance that George will be back for the week-end. If so, I shall be happy, needless to say. If not, we shall be spared another farewell, which will be not a bad thing, either.

The telephone and telegraph companies will be able to point to the week of August 6-13 as that in which they made their profit for the year 1943, I feel sure. I shall be glad when this week is far enough behind me that I shall not jump instinctively for the phone, knowing that it is probably news of one sort or another. After a while one begins to think the bells are ringing inside one's head.

Chris expects to be joining George next month, which is one of the many reasons for my desire to get home at the end of the month.

Feel like a million dollars, in spite of the fact that hours for sleeping have been few and far between. The teeth seem to have settled down, and everything points to the fact that one of them has quietly died. As soon as I am sure that George is not going to be here, I shall go into the hospital and have the wisdom tooth dealt with in the approved manner. Probably Monday or so.

RCAF Operations, SPB
Dartmouth, N.S.
Aug. 17th, 1943

I hope to be home on the twenty-ninth of August or so, for about two weeks. That is, if all goes well.

George Buch came back. He was in town late Thursday night, even as I was writing to you on the Graveyard Shift. I went into town Friday morning to sleep at the room and to await a telegram from George. Had just drifted to sleep about eleven a.m. when the phone rang. So no sleep that day!

I had to work Saturday morning, but the officer in charge was most kind and I was given the rest of the week-end off. Friday night the boys had a party. Three of George's friends were with him, and three Nursing Sisters and me.

Saturday night we all went to the Lord Nelson for dinner and then out to the old Mess. Since the Battalion had gone, the music was provided by an Air Force Band. We left before midnight – a thing we have never done.

Sunday I went to church with George and the three boys and we met the Nursing Sisters afterwards for dinner at the Hotel. The boys packed hurriedly and left in a station-wagon right after dinner, about three – for the last time.

I came back to the Station at once to report for work, but was given the evening off, since my forty-eight was not yet over. I worked yesterday morning (Monday) and in the afternoon I appeared for the oft-postponed wisdom-tooth extraction.

I had been postponing this visit to the dentist until the day after I was almost certain that George had sailed on the Queen Elizabeth *for overseas duty. As I sat in the chair with my mouth frozen right down to my toes, the drilling, hammering and chiselling began in earnest, and rivulets of tears started coursing down my cheeks. Noting my distress, Major Matchett, the splendid Army dentist assigned to the Base, immediately stopped his work and asked, "Am I hurting you ?" My muffffled reply, through cotton wool*

51

and freezing was, " No, I'm just lonesome," and indicated he should keep on with the extraction of my wisdom tooth. The WD assisting him then explained that the patient had just said good-bye to her fiancéand the Major was able to continue, knowing that my tears were not a by-product of his handiwork.

In a sense, this incident points to the fact that while we might crab about the food, complain about the lack of clean sheets, or be furious if someone borrowed our curlers without asking, when it came to situations that called for inner fortitude, we all tried to keep our emotions in check. Your fiancé may have shipped out for Britain and your impacted wisdom tooth was about to be removed, but tears were not in order. There was a war on, after all.

I am writing from a very comfy hospital bed. This is a much nicer (because larger) hospital than the one at Rockcliffe. I'm in a ward with several friends and the girls run in from Barracks often. We lack nothing. I probably shall be here only another day or two. I started calling out for solid food today and they are suspicious that perhaps I am fit for work!

The tooth is a beauty. I'd put it in a glass of water if I thought the fairies would leave a quarter for it. I won't settle for less! The only part that was bad was when the dentist took a chisel and a hammer and banged away as though he were cutting stone – a new experience for me. Have caught up quite a lot on sleep, which I needed, and feel A-1.

Wish I could get overseas, but that is not possible, so we in the ward have decided to strike a medal for those veterans of the Second Great War who have seen Active Service in Halifax. The medal will have fish on the obverse side, and an umbrella on the reverse!

One of the Nursing Sisters is going over with the boys and you should hear the amount of luggage she intends to take – including a bicycle. We tried to convince her that a Canadian bicycle would not be allowed in England, where they have left-hand drive, and at first she was inclined to believe us.

RCAF Dartmouth
Aug. 21, 1943

The postal system here leaves much to be desired and the mail has gone from one section to another, until I finally walked a couple of miles to pick it up in a remote corner of some God-forsaken spot on the Station.

Have had three letters and a wire from George. He is still in Nova Scotia. I can't help hoping that I shall not see him again. Sounds hard of me, I suppose, but we have had such glorious times together that I would rather he remembers those than yet another series of good-byes.

Chris is now on his Embarkation Leave, and if I can get home on the 28th or 29th, as I plan, I shall see him. They are talking of giving us our "trade test" for Clerk Ops on the 30th, which will upset still further the nice little plans I had made. However, I may yet go home on the 31st or the 1st of September and perhaps Chris will still be around. There is little hope of seeing him on the way through here, but you cannot go around saying good-bye to everyone indefinitely and for days at a time. I firmly believe that everything works out for the best sooner or later, and am trying not to worry about it.

The long-awaited two weeks leave finally became a reality; however, after the train trip to and from Montreal and doing the rounds of family and friends -including Marion Strang – before I knew it, it was time to report back to the base in Dartmouth. My brother, Chris, was still in the vicinity and might leave any day for overseas, so at least we had the prospect of seeing each other occasionally until his posting came due. However, I was not prepared for the unexpectedly cold temperatures that had already set in on my return to Nova Scotia in mid-September.

Dartmouth, N.S.
RCAF S.P.B.,
Sun. p.m. Sept. 12, 1943

Back in the groove again, as though I had never been away. Yes, Graveyard Shift! We're all wrapped up in blankets, in a vain effort to shut out the atmospheric conditions. There's a fire in the stove, but since I'm on the opposite side of the room, it's not much help. I shudder to think of winter's icy hand, if this is September.

The trip back down was pleasant and I met a number of people I knew – Mrs. Neilson, of Quebec, whose daughter Helen, is our Senior Messing Officer in Eastern Air Command. Helen got on the train at Moncton to meet her mother. Also in the same car were a Captain in Dad's outfit and a Major who has just come back from Kiska. All very interesting.

I was in bed by ten o'clock and heard nothing until the second call for breakfast the next morning. Your fudge filled in chinks between meals and I alternately read and slept during the morning.

It's the rule of war that our meetings be framed by their endings – the incident named by its limitation – and I'm just one of the fortunate ones who can get home once in a while, thus breaking the persistent spell of the present.

I went back on shift Saturday and then spent the evening in the railway station trying to locate my forty pounds of luggage, which includes two new shirts, three pairs of new pyjamas, a new pair of rubbers, a number of books, and goodness knows what else. Travelling, I always end up with more stuff than

S/O (later Flt. Officer) Helen Neilson, M.B.E. Chief Messing Officer, RCAF Eastern Air Command 1943-45.

I started with. Somehow finding the duffle bag was quite a chore. Have you ever tried to find a piece of baggage that has several thousand brothers, all identical ? However, all was well in the end.

Sunday morning I worked again and Chris phoned from Windsor, N.S. at noon. He was able to come down on the five o'clock bus, so we had supper at the Jones' place and back he went at seven. Chris says the food is pretty good and the mosquitoes aren't as numerous as when George was there. We were two mighty homesick bunnies, though neither of us said so, and it was mighty nice to see each other.

Our shift finishes at seven-thirty in the morning and we are on again at five, so tomorrow – or today, rather – is a day for sleeping. We work again Tuesday afternoon and in the evening we're all going out to a nearby lake for a swim and a corn-roast. And so it goes.

I had half-hoped that it would not be too soon for a letter from George, but I guess it is. There is no posting list, either, so I guess Dartmouth is our home for a while yet. I must finish off.

Later... Finish off! I did that, all right. Fell asleep in my blanket. Five A.M. now and dawn just breaking. Br-r-r! Long red flannels and ski boots are indicated.

During the latter part of our stint at the Sea Plane Base, we were all impatiently awaiting word of our next posting. After completion of our Ops B exam in Dartmouth, several of us were slated to attend an Officers' Training Course in Toronto, however there was a waiting list, and no indication of when those who had qualified for the Course might expect to be sent off. A Newfoundland posting was still a possibility, whereas an overseas posting was merely a distant dream. In the interval, we continued to make the best of things as they stood, and to live in hope.

It's on a night like this that I dream of a land where they have pleasant Septembers. Where the leaves turn before they are blown off, and no one's feet are ever, ever wet. Where skies are blue once in a while, and the sun shines between the clouds, and not beyond them!

I was up at Windsor. Had a shift off yesterday and by tearing off at noon, I got up and back with a night in the town and still managed to get back to work by five today. The Jones' happened to be going that way unexpectedly, so I drove up with them yesterday afternoon. Chris met me and took me to the Mess for the evening.

I was able to get a room at a very pleasant tourist place in Windsor, and saw Chris again this morning then returned on the noon train. I have never seen such a train. The engine wanders away at each station. Someone has to go and get it and bring it back and hitch it up. I'm all for originality and so forth, but when an engine takes it into its head to be independent and leaves its train at the least excuse, that's too much!

I bought a beautiful pair of rubber boots in Windsor. They're size seven -in Men's size, and I think I'll have to tie a piece of cord on each to help lift them with every step. But there is lots of room for socks and they are weatherproof. All I have to worry about now is making sure that I have a dry pair of socks every day. If it's not one thing, it's another.

I've been to a couple of the Station movies this week. *The Floor's In*, which was poor and *Forever and a Day* which was better. Apart from that, it's been a case of the nose pretty much to the grindstone. There is talk of changing our shifts again, in order to let us work a week at a time on the same shift. I shall be glad if it comes through. Maybe I'll get some breakfast occasionally. All this week I've either been sleeping or working and food is a good thing in its own way, don't you think?

No change of linen yet. I thought when I went away on Leave that this would be the month. Everyone stripped their beds while I was away -but there were no clean replacement sheets, so I am the only one in the Barracks with sheets on my bed and my friends fight over who is to sleep in them. A case of Goldilock's Baby Bear ... "Someone's Been Sleeping in My Bed!" but I don't mind, as long as the bed is unoccupied when I stagger in after the Graveyard.

Wasn't it the twenty-sixth of July that I came over here? I've washed the sheets myself twice since then, but they don't ever dry, so what's the use?

We have to wear running-shoes in the Ops Room now. It's hard on the arches and very cold, but dulls the noise. Anything for efficiency. What crocks we will be, when the war is over! No teeth, no arches, stiff shoulders! We'll probably all fall down the day the peace is signed – if not before! (Don't take me too seriously!)

Letters from England this week. My heart went over to London two weeks ago and life seems to be colour and warmth and light... I had a letter from George's Aunt Olga, too, telling of his visit. He had had the week-end off and spent it with her.

S.P.B. RCAF,
Dartmouth, N.S.
Oct. 2nd, 1943

The work we had been doing in Operations made us well aware of the presence of German submarines in the vicinity and whenever they were detected in the Gulf of St. Lawrence or near the East Coast, their positions were immediately plotted. By the autumn of 1943 the number of enemy subs had begun to diminish as the Allies gained the upper hand, but crossing the Atlantic remained a very risky prospect as there were still ships being sunk en route.

The past few days have not been uneventful, as you have seen by the headlines. Once in a while we feel that our job is worth something, but even so, the dreadful toll in the Atlantic reminds us that tired eyes are not for sleeping.

Pat Moore, my former room-mate from the B.W.I. who is now stationed in P.E.I. was here on a "96". It was while she was here that she heard that her uncle, Lieut-Commander de Freitas, had been lost on the *St. Croix*. He had been here in Halifax in July, and we three girls had seen a great deal of him. We were on board the ship just before she sailed. He was a peach of a chap and it's a rotten business.

I'm on a "48" just now and came in to see Pat off on the train this morning. I'm going up to Windsor this afternoon to spend the week-end. I have to be back for the Graveyard Shift Monday night and shall be working nights all this week.

With the new shifts going ahead, there is just a chance that I can get to Montreal or Quebec on my next long week-end, about the 24th. I'd have a day, and – if the weather is good enough to fly – perhaps longer. There are so many if's, that I shall wait a few days to see how things work out, before I can plan anything.

A Kit Inspection has come upon us – scheduled for early in the week. My overshoes, tin hat, greatcoat and numerous other trifles are still at the room in Halifax and my kit is far from complete. At last the powers-that-be are to find out the Awful Truth! Perhaps now I shall be issued with a few things I need. I've been trying for weeks to have my name put on Kitting Parade.

Back on the Graveyard for a whole week. You should see us, trotting down to the Shack at eleven-thirty p.m. all carrying blankets and books and food. We take turns sleeping. I usually read until about three and then stretch out until five and from then on, write. Breakfast at six-fifteen, then the Dawn Patrol follows and we're through at eight. It's quite something, going to sleep on a large flat table, sloping at a slight angle. Who said, "I could sleep on a board"? Well, we do! Whoever is awake stokes the fire – one more qualification for the return to civilian life. And I'm a moderately good shoveller now.

I have a horrid feeling that perhaps that old posting list will loom up soon and if it's Gander Bay, Nfld. it'll be for a year, so they say. Wish I could think that a year and the duration were synonymous. I wouldn't mind a year anywhere if I knew the war would be over.

During the latter part of our Dartmouth stint at the Sea Plane Base we were all impatiently awaiting word of our next Posting. Several of us were slated to attend an Officers' Training Course in Toronto, however there was a waiting list, and no indication of when those who had qualified for the Course might expect to be sent off. A Newfoundland Posting was also a possibility, while an Overseas Posting was merely a distant dream. In the interval, we continued to make the best of things as they stood, and to live in hope.

History was made this week! Remember my tale of woe about the sheets? I took mine to the Chinese laundry in desperation and then on Monday the Air Force came through with nice fresh linen. We were about to suggest that the letters "S.P.B." (on our address) might stand for "Sheets Positively Banned". But we are happy now. Five of us have been moved to another, quieter barrack-room, and this, plus the sheets, is almost too much. I had a very peculiar mattress on my other bed. This one is lumpy, but soft. And a Room With a View!

Had a pleasant time at Windsor over the week-end. Chris suddenly got five days' leave just as I arrived, so he went home. I stayed in Windsor anyway and the lads took me to the Mess Saturday and Sunday. Sunday night they escorted me to the bus, only to find that there were no seats. So I checked in at the Tourist House again and caught the 4 a.m train (or overtook it – nearer the truth!) Shocked the good people of Windsor, I think, starting out at that hour of the morning. But night and day are the same to an Airwoman.

This has been completed at two a.m. Guess I'll improve my posture on the table!

The Inspector-General is due here on his annual tour of inspection next week, so we scrub and polish and wax and clean, and in between times we drill...and drill...and drill. No passes are being issued this week and we are Confined to Barracks every night. Ah yes, it's fun – of a sort. I can't say I approve of the idea of such hectic preparations. How much better to have the camp cleared up regularly, not annually; but a lowly airwoman takes her pail and a can of Johnson's floor wax and says, "Yes, Ma'am", and goes – meekly! The drill is quite something; wearing our tin helmets and bearing our gas-masks, on the alert. I wish the I.G. would come tomorrow. If he has any sense of humour at all, he'd enjoy this intimate glimpse of industry!

Spent the week-end at Windsor. Perfectly heavenly weather. I take it all back. Autumn in Nova Scotia is enough to erase all recollection of fog and mud. The colours are glorious and the hills all aflame. Here and there the frost has not yet touched the valleys and there is still greenery. Neither northern Ontario nor Quebec can beat the scenery I saw this past week-end.

I have an invitation to the Windsor dance at Christmas! Cutting out paper dolls is the activity for this week. Chris had a wonderful week at home and brought back the news that everyone is well.

Had a permanent today, so I am very curly, and very short! The Corporal will like it on Parade tomorrow – no hair hiding my collar. And if the Corporal likes it, so will the Sergeant and so on – right up to the Inspector-General himself.

Also today (this I hardly dare tell you) I had a medical to see if I am fit for Overseas Duty. No, not Newfoundland – the Real Thing...the Blessed Plot... the Realm – England! My name, with several others has been sent to AFHQ and one of these weeks perhaps I shall be one of six from here. The chances are even. Superstition almost forbids me to write or speak of it, but it has been under my hat for so long now that I'm ready to burst!

The medical exam produced evidence that though I have lost weight, I have the approved number of red corpuscles, which is rather important. I didn't tell the M.O. that I've put on eight of the ten pounds I lost in August, so have only two more to go.

It's five-thirty a.m. now so I think I'll wander over to the Mess and see if they're giving away any free coupons in the porridge today...

No news of my posting! But lots of other chatter. I have been surrounded by shades of Winnipeg this week – if you could call Mary Taunton and Sheila (Strang) shades! [*Sheila Strang was a distant cousin of Marion Strang's husband*

and hailed from Vancouver.] Cousin Mary Taunton has had her Leave, and is temporarily a resident of the "Y" Depot. She and several other WD officers from Rockliffe have been posted to take a special course in Intelligence and Photography, and they will be posted to RCAF Bomber Squadrons Overseas "upon successful completion of same". I am so glad for Mary's sake. We have all been hoping for a long time that she'd get a break. She has done a wonderful job at Rockcliffe, where others might merely have been bored and let it go at that. It's strange how differently one can react to one's officers. I suppose it's a matter of personal magnetism plus the fact that giving a little bit more makes the difference between discipline and morale.

Mary telephoned me Wednesday night and Thursday we went to the hotel, had a drink with Sheila and then dinner. The old Inspector-General is seeing to it that this airwoman's spare time is well-looked-after, but I was able to get to town this morning for breakfast and lunch with Sheila. A most side-splitting day, to put it mildly! Sheila has been down on Temporary Duty and returns to Rockcliffe tomorrow. She was inspecting Operations in order to see what kind of gals they want down here. Between crawling out after her through the hotel windows onto a roof to see the view and listening to her accounts of numerous experiences, it was quite a morning.

Sheila came over to see our workshop yesterday and she has been browsing around all the secret places of Eastern Air Command. She tells me she has nearly ruined her eyes trying to read the posting list on the Wing-Commander's desk upside down. Having talked with our Commandant, she agrees that if I don't make the grade, it'll be because the O/C "worries" about my health. Damn it!

I expect to be seeing Mary Taunton again shortly. There's no knowing how long she'll be here. Chris is still at Windsor, so perhaps they'll cross together.

Life on the Station is just as I said in my last letter. It's a good thing I'm feeling strong (eating my corn-flakes). We've been spending our mornings working, our afternoons on a two-hour parade, – simply standing – and on shift in the evening. But I feel like a million. Probably because we sleep like logs when we do get to bed, and have to eat as much heavy food as we can pack away. The sun on the parade-square is hot and my face is a light beet-colour. We'll all be happy when the Inspector-General has come and gone. Tonight we had to scrub every inch of the Shack. It reminded me of Rockcliffe days in a way.

This has been written in a terrific rush. It's almost midnight and after a trip to the Mess for a plate o'beans, I shall trudge up to the Barracks to flop on the nearest bunk for six hours.

P.S. Don't know why I neglected to mail this letter, but in any case can now add the latest – that I am to report to the "Y" Depot two weeks after the third of November. I don't know whether I'm on my heels or my head, but nothing matters! Sorry not to be home this week-end, but in view of the situation, shall see you the week of November 3rd.

Have come down from my cloud long enough to buy (a) some flash-light batteries and (b) three collar-pins. Why the latter, I don't know. Of all the things I need, I need collar-pins the least! Our entire conversation consists of the amount of baggage we're allowed to take...(rumours vary) and what we'll need. My chief worry is stationery! It's hard to get air mail paper over there, according to George, and I can see myself loaded down with bags full of unwritten letters.

The Inspector-General's Parade was finally held yesterday. It was just about final too. That's the word for it. The Inspection alone took two hours, to say nothing of the long march up the hill, the General Salute, the March Past and all the rest of the fanfare. I kept telling myself, all during the long stand, that it was probably my last big Parade in Canada. When the I.G. finally told us we could "Stand Easy", we thought our knees would surely break, but by some miracle they didn't. I had worked on the Graveyard Shift the night before and the Parade took all afternoon, so I was in great form by bed-time last night!

Having nothing better to do with my time I wandered into the dental office at noon today, to inquire after the health of one of my wisdom teeth – the fourth and only remaining one. Before I could say anything it was out, so that's something else off my mind. The minute the authorities realize that you're departing, they make good use of what little time remains to finish you off. I think I'll steer clear of the M.O. He might want my appendix or a lung or two.

There certainly have never been prouder, happier girls than we are. The fact that Canada thinks we're useful enough to send to England really thrills me. I still don't know what I've done to deserve this break, when there are so many others who have been wanting to go for so long.

We're all trotting around with little lists which contain everything from long underwear and a scarf to perfume and an alarm clock. We all say cheerfully that we'll take as many civilian clothes as we can, but I foresee a day of reckoning when we start to repack.

It's so exciting! How are we ever going to live through the next two months or so, without bursting? Did I tell you what I did when I heard the news? I was sewing my Props badges on one of my uniforms, and – trying to be cool – went blithely on sewing until I had sewed right through both sleeves, and couldn't put my arms into my tunic!

Can't find my own pen, which upsets me muchly. It would have to happen now, on top of everything. I think I know where it is, but a lot of help that is on the Graveyard Shift!

Ball-point pens were as yet unknown, so everyone in the Services used a fountain-pen. This called for a bottle of ink somewhere in the vicinity, since a pen's reservoir had a limited capacity. Carrying about a bottle of ink presented its own hazards and bitter experience taught us to avoid packing an ink bottle in our dunnage bags. Service Clubs provided inkwells and pens with nibs, so that a letter could be written using the 'dip and write' method; however, at the best of times, letter-writing was a relatively complicated operation. Small wonder that pencils often served as a reliable substitute.

Mary Taunton isn't around now and I don't think Chris is either, which only serves to make me all the more anxious to be on my way. Cables from George have been coming thick and fast. He is with the 1st Battalion now, which makes him very happy. Wish I knew where the 1st is, though. Not that it would do me any good to know – my geography of England being what it is.

Have "Canada" sewn up on my uniforms now – the biggest thrill of my air force career (which is limited, I admit!).

With that strange way that life has of turning up with the right thing at the auspicious moment, an avalanche of English mail has fallen into my lap this week. News from one lad was that a letter I wrote last May had followed him through various theatres of war and back to England. A letter from another chap, was written from the same camp where George is stationed. (I am wondering if he has met George yet!). A communication from a third, that I am now to address him in Africa.

Shall not bore you with a play-by-play account of the various inspections which we are undergoing. It is a little hard to get a full day's sleep. Officers and N.C.O.s come looking at our belongings, to see whether we have a full kit or not, and I find it only slightly amusing to spring to attention, half-awake, in my pyjamas. I never know the answers to half the questions they ask.

Have not recovered, either, from the medical officer's interview. He asked me how it was that I appeared to have escaped my injections! There is – or was – still no record of any needles on my documents. Believe me, I talked *fast*! I'd never go through that affair a third time for anything. The efficiency of the Service! How I love it!

Am looking forward to next week more than I can say. Two weeks away from bedlam seems like reprieve. All I ask is that no one (not even you, please!)

mention beans or beef! This will be my last fling, complete with bath tub, bed at night, fresh milk – and sheets ... the fundamental things of life! At four a.m., one's dreams (I can't call 'em day-dreams) tend to be of very simple things.

Dartmouth, N.S.
Oct. 31st, 1943

I'm nearing the end of the last couple of a long line of Graveyards. Soon I'll be back to the normal life of sleepless days and ordinary sleepful nights. Am just about packed, have a few more details to see to on Monday, then work Monday night and shall be on the Montreal train at the crack of dawn Tuesday – I hope. So look out, Montreal. Here I come!

I thought Chris had gone – but not so! He telephoned on Thursday night. Poor fish! I feel so sorry for them there...We have been busy at work what with one thing and another. Practice makes perfect, but at what price.

Did I tell you I had dinner with Helen Neilson this week. She is very amusing, is Helen. Can't get a berth on the train for Tuesday night, so I guess we sleep sitting up – in the best Ops Room style. This week of Graveyard will put me in practice.

> *Our families were surprised, of course, to hear that we were coming home for yet another fortnight, since we were unable to convey to them that we were on Embarkation Leave and about to ship out. I think the full impact of leaving didn't really hit home until we were on the train heading back to Halifax and facing the prospect of boarding a ship and heading out across the Atlantic. As we rattled through the November rain in New Brunswick, I thought of the opening lines of Canon Scott's* The Great War As I Saw It *where he described sailing out of the St. Lawrence into the Gulf in the First World War and how "the green arms of the hills encompassed us, as though Canada were reluctant to let us go..."*

"Y" Depot, Halifax
Thurs., Nov. 18th, 1943
noon

Have just time to write to you before we dash for lunch. The train trip from Montreal was very pleasant. A merry crowd. Motley and noisy at times. Ate and slept and slept and talked.

We arrived at one a.m. today with much red tape and a search for blankets. It must have been two when we got to bed. Then Parade at eight this morning. Winter is here, too, let me tell you!

All morning we spent in communion with the Sergeant about our documents. We shall be busy during the next little while. Tried to pretend this morning when I awoke that if I kept my eyes shut I could believe I was anywhere but here! Not so. The place is just as it was when I was here before.

"Y" Depot
Halifax
Mon. Nov. 22, 1943

These are dreadfully sloppy letters these days, but no table, no time,- no nuffin'! We just have to make the best of what opportunities we have.

Many of us spent the weekend in bed. We were free to do as we pleased and that seemed the best thing, in view of the fact that the return to Spartan life has just about ruined us all. I remember very little of what happened after Saturday noon. I just tucked myself into my rat's nest beneath four blankets, and emerged only for meals.

We have been issued cutlery and mess tins. My mess-tin has seen service in another war. I hope I may keep it as a souvenir after this one. It's round – the two halves fit together and there is a handle inside, with which to convert the thing into a frying-pan if need be.

Also now own a gas-cape, anti-gas equipment, ointment, first aid dressings and water-canteen. My knap-sack is packed with slacks, a sweater, my heaviest pyjamas, a flash-light, malted milk tablets, heavy socks and my sheepskin slippers [*a hand-made gift from Marion Strang]. By the time I have on my greatcoat, haversack, water-canteen, blanket roll, gas-cape roll and carry my rain-coat and dunnage bag, I shall be fit for the Highland Fling – I don't think!

My chamois jacket is very warm. It's flannel-lined, and covered with grey silk – quite posh! Must dash off for parade again. You likely will hear from me again in a day or so. .

"Y" Depot, RCAF
Tues., Nov. 23, 1943
7:30 a.m.

This is written in wild haste...

I wish you could see my luggage. There's just enough left over to fill a small trunk. I was afraid this would happen! But the hand-made slippers are packed. Thanks again.

There has been very little time for homesickness, and no time for anything else. As I said to someone today, "If you take even two minutes off just to go to the John you miss five parades, three rumours and a meal..." We are physical wrecks – all of us! But we'll recover.

And now I must make my message speedy. I hope you keep well, and I pray continually that your ship will come in. [*This in reference to Marion Strang receiving word of her son, Kenneth, who had been taken prisoner at Hong Kong.*]

A funny thing happened last night. We had all tucked in and I was coughing myself to sleep about one a.m. Just as I was dropping off, there was a tremendous noise at the door and then silence. You won't often get me to admit that this kind of thing occurs, but one of the girls had been celebrating her last free night and had returned tiddly enough to fall over the fire extinguisher and set it off. I got up, found my flashlight and went over.

She wasn't hurt, but she couldn't find her hat. I waded around in the water, finally found it, then got her down as far as what she claimed to be her bunk. There were already two people in the double-decker, so we found another bed, which turned out to be the right one. My chief concern was that we would awaken the other thirty-eight sleeping beauties – which was the least of *her* worries! I retired gracefully (?) then and dried myself off. Fifteen minutes later I went back to see how she was navigating. She was still trying to hang up her greatcoat on a hook that wasn't there, but finally she did get to bed. I admit to having assisted my friends in such circumstances before, but never until now have I had to cope with a discharged fire-extinguisher!

And now I must jump into my long blue underwear for the first time. Duty calls, as ne'er before. Sorry I can't call you up. I had looked forward to it, however I'm sure you will understand.

PART FOUR

Overseas at Last
November 1943 – January 1944

Although by the late autumn of 1943, the Battle of the North Atlantic was slowly but surely being won, if it occurred to any of us that crossing the ocean during the cold, short days of late November might involve a degree of risk, we quickly put the thought out of our minds.

R.C.A.F. Overseas
Dec. 5th, 1943

The last week before we left Halifax was entirely grim. The Corporal's idea was to let us stand for three hours at a time, morning and afternoon, in the streaming rain. . . waiting for only-she-knew-what. Cold barracks, cold water and a cold in the head! There was one awful half-hour when we had a Medical and I coughed at the wrong time and had to wait with a crowd of others to have a thermometer put in my mouth. It turned out I was all right, so away we went.

Orders kept coming, to countermand previous orders concerning the subject of blankets. First we were to take a pair overseas, then we were not. Since they are the obvious thing to put in the bottom of a kit-bag, it meant a series of repacks – and each time I seemed to have more stuff left over than I had had the previous time. The final order was that we take the blankets with us, but in the meantime we spent a good deal of time trotting back and forth to Equipment and before we were through, we met each other on return trips. The smart ones were the ones who got behind in their schedule, for in the end they missed a couple of countermands.

The trip began with a bang. With all our equipment on, we couldn't do anything but stand. No room to bend in the middle and sit down! All was fairly comfortable until we started on with our kit-bags. I walked backwards up the gang-plank dragging mine... (Dragging is so good for the bottom of the bag!) I also left two puddles of rye in the shed. The 40 oz. bottle was well-packed, but the cap got nicked by an adjacent tin and it all leaked out. So I'll never know whether it was "Good to the Last Drop" or not. There wasn't a drop left. Right through all my belongings, since the bottle was at the top.

As soon as we got to our cabin, I had to unpack everything, and hang the stuff up to dry. Harris Tweed is quite improved, I may say, by the scent of rye, but how unpopular I was in the cabin! Nothing we could do would dispel the odor. I suspect it helped to make two of our number deathly sick. Certainly it didn't improve the atmosphere – adding rye to an already stuffy stateroom! It was dark soon after we boarded and the port-holes were then closed, of course.

When we boarded the Mauritania in Halifax, we were given cabins on the top deck, next to those occupied by the officers. There were seven girls in our cabin, with three double-decker berths crammed into what would have been a single cabin in peace-time. My companions-at-sea included Sgts. Marg Norum, Paddy Seecombe and Zella Stade, Corporals Jean Houston and Jean Jamieson, both of whom had been on the West coast, plus Airwomen Muriel Allen and Mona Murdock. With our accumulation of kit-bags, haversacks, gas masks, respirators and bulky life preservers, space was at a premium. Due to the shortness of daylight hours, black-out conditions were required by the early afternoon.

Aside from a Life-boat Drill every morning, we were at liberty to wander at will. To work up an appetite, many of us spent a good deal of time walking the deck, in the firm belief that eating well helped to ward off sea-sickness. Whether or not it actually spared anyone, we felt as if we were living proof of the truth of this particular snippet of sea-lore.

We girls had staterooms usually reserved for officers. There were seven of us and only six bunks; so we each took one turn on the deck. We ate in the Officers' Mess. Breakfast at nine and dinner at seven-thirty were our shift-hours, with soup and crackers at one. Mona Murdock, Helen Woodcroft and I were the three at our table who always turned up. I ate huge meals. Two helpings of everything in sight, after walking the decks. Five-course meals with great, hard,

RMS MAURETANIA – a Cunard liner, built in Birkenhead, England in 1939 and converted to wartime use for the transport of troops overseas.

crusty rolls and butter – even oranges and apples galore. As some of the others got sicker and sicker, Mona and I seemed to get fitter and fitter, until I know we must have tried the others with our enthusiasm.

To break up the day a bit (*not* because the sea air made us sleepy!) we turned in for a couple of hours each day after lunch. We had the use of the officers' sun-deck, which was most pleasant. We couldn't have had kinder treatment all the way over. Everyone was very attentive.

The part that tickled Mona about the rye incident was that I wouldn't wear my new slippers the night in barracks that the fire-extinguisher tipped over. And then they got soaked in whiskey anyway. So now they have been christened! Mona goes around telling people that I won't wear my slippers in water, but just try me on rye! That moment was Life's Darkest, when I lost that bottle. The scotch and a couple of small gins were mercifully preserved.

There were vast numbers of friends on board – some of Chris's brother-officers and a Colonel from Dad's regiment, who was very paternal, and tens of others whom I had either trained with or had known before. The entertainers put on their show for us and altogether we had a roaring good time. Some of the R.A.F. boys were teaching us to play a game called "Solo" and for the first time in my life I got thirteen trumps – to my own consternation and theirs. Too bad we weren't gambling, eh? We next were introduced to a brand of Poker and again this New Girl came out on top. It makes you suspect the Dealer, doesn't it?

One of the funniest things that happened to Mona and me on board was on the night that one of the girls turned up for the first time for dinner after several days in her cabin. We were talking enthusiastically about how good the roast duckling was, when a green face suddenly spoke up and said that if I didn't stop talking about food, she'd throw a tea-pot at me. I was so surprised that I shut up! She's one of our N.C.O.s and we've called her "Tea-pot" ever since; but she was really serious.

Some of the girls were down the whole way over. What a chore to have to cope with baggage at this end! I have never been so completely exhausted as I was after that load. Whew!

Our draft of fifty Clerk Ops arrived in England on the first of December, 1943 and we were taken overnight by train to Bournemouth on the south coast. From there we were posted to our respective Stations. We were very keen to get to our work and it would not be an exaggeration to say that we not only assumed we would be fully employed, but also that that we had actually come over to help SAVE England. It came as a great blow when the Commanding Officer of all the WDs in England, Wing Officer K. Walker, made a special trip from London to give us the bad news that we'd been sent overseas by mistake – a communications error between London and Ottawa. London had requested "Clerks General" and Ottawa had understood "Clerks Operational."

Once ashore, however, we were welcomed despite the circumstances of our arrival. Wing Officer Walker told us that it was like pulling teeth to persuade Ottawa to release any WDs for overseas duty. When the error came to light, it was decided that the less said about the situation, the better for all concerned. In other words we were welcome and needed. Her parting words were, " Now, most of you will have to come to London, re-train and then muster to trades other than your own..." Eventually twenty-five or so re-mustered to trades such as Photography, and the rest of us were posted either to Number Six RCAF Bomber Group in Yorkshire or to the RCAF Fighter Station at Digby in Lincolnshire.

The R.C.A.F. Band played for us as we docked. They played all afternoon on the quay.... "Roll Out The Barrel" and "Moonlight Cocktail" and "Land of Hope and Glory". . . The boys threw cigarettes and chocolate bars to them and to the civilians on the shore. One of those scenes one doesn't forget.

We were given the American "Iron Ration" – three different units of it – to eat on the train. It's very good stuff, but we didn't need to use it. As soon as we got onto the train, the boys came through with great hunks of bread, "butter" [*margarine*], cheese, bully beef, beans and potatoes and tea. We had to sit up all night, but the time passed very quickly. We played cards and swapped stories and amused ourselves with all the novelties of an English train. The "facilities" amused us. A complicated system of knobs, bells, buttons, chains, plugs and pedals, and a tin wash-basin that comes out of the wall and hits you when you aren't looking. Guaranteed to confuse the enemy, to say nothing of a harmless stranger!

We were met by WAAFs, who brought us to our billets. We are comfortably established in hotel-billets, in a city by the sea.[*The Bournemouth Reception Centre*] We had breakfast – a good meal, truly – then a wash, and when the others went to bed, I went off in search of new sights. Four of us ended up by meeting unexpectedly at the Knights of Columbus Hut.

George had just finished a course in London and had three days' Leave. He came down the next day and what a time we had! He had simply said he would come down after lunch. I was a bit puzzled as to when "after lunch" might be. I could give him no useful advice about how to reach me, so after duty I started off to look for the station. An R.C.A.F. Sergeant found me a cab and we went together. He showed me how to put a penny in a slot to buy a ticket admitting me to the platform, and we waited for a London train.

By this time the blackout was on. Picture us, if you can. The Sergeant looking for someone he had never seen, but who was said to look "wonderful" and I, eager, but unable to keep track of even the Sergeant in the pitch dark – much less sort out George if he turned up among the thousands. I was just beginning to realize what a stupid thing I had done, to leave the only place in town where I knew where I was, to wander off in a blacked-out station, while George might have disembarked at the other station and be looking for me there, when suddenly I caught sight of him, just as he saw me.

We got a cab, delivered the Sergeant to his destination and then went on to George's hotel. I had been lucky to get him a room. This is a great peace-time summer resort, but with the war on, many places are closed. A lot have been taken over for billets and the remainder are crowded. We were both amazed that for the equivalent of $2.25 a day he had a room, breakfast, very good service and an electric heater in the room.

I had my first exciting ride on a double-decker bus ... and I do mean exciting! I have the distinct impression that in this city there is no "right" side of the road – there's only the middle. Everything travels at a clip and I feel as though I'm taking my life in my hands crossing the street. In time we will get used to the traffic differences.

Telephone kiosks are to be found on almost every corner. Put two pennies in, ring a bell, give the number, press another button, and there you are!

The sirens went while we were out for dinner, but we heard nothing, and the "All Clear" sounded shortly. Coming back in the blackout is eerie to the uninitiated like me, and for a girl it's not good! I shall not be out alone at night, I can assure you.

I asked our WAAF Sergeant whether or not I had to be at Church Parade today. I had tried – and she had tried for me – to get Leave to go up to London, but no can do at the moment. She had said that in any case she'd give me all the time off she could and this Parade was the start. Officially, the Sergeant said, the Parade was compulsory for everyone except Christian Scientists and there was a lecture afterwards, as well. Then she took me aside and said, looking off into space, "When I say 'Christian Scientists fall – out!' if you don't fall out, then it's your own fault."

I was on the Parade Square at 8 a.m. and away by five after. George collected me at ten and, as it was too early to go to a Service then, we went to a restaurant and had tea. It's surprising how soon we have begun the tea-drinking habit! We actually have a break morning and afternoon so we can dash to one of the many canteens or restaurants for tea and a bun. Always a bun!

Later we went to St. Peter's Church, not far from where I live. The Archdeacon of Winchester came to preach and the service was beautiful. They have a Boys' choir and lovely music.

It was a pretty wonderful week-end. To see George again, after three months (which is really not long in war-time) was great, especially when we had expected to be apart so much longer. We hope to be married about the middle of January, if we can both get Leave then. George can't get Leave before, and I don't want to take mine until he can. It will be quick and quiet – probably in London. I do hope Chris gets here in time to give me away.

We girls have been busy getting documented (between dates!). Each of us had an individual, personal interview with Wing Officer K. Walker, the senior WD Officer, United Kingdom. She broke the news to us that we came over as the result of a horrible mistake! We aren't really needed at all here for the sort of work we have been trained for. So we can't "save" England, or beat back the Germans or anything. But they do need "other types". There are more than enough WAAF and RAF in Ops who have had experience ever since the early days of the Battle of Britain, so the last thing needed is a fresh crop of inexperienced Canucks, but they do need personnel for other jobs. A great deal of vagueness about our future, anyhow.

"The Kilt" is evidently quite a novelty in this particular locality and Americans, especially, have been asking George what he is! One U.S. Sergeant confided today that he had seen a *picture* of a kilt once. Last night a couple of Yanks tried to pick us both up in the blackout. They got quite a surprise when it finally dawned on George and he turned around and spoke to them in a deep voice!

My cousin, Mary Taunton, now in Yorkshire wrote to me. She is enjoying her work and I have her address, so perhaps I shall soon see her.

Most of us thought we knew what to expect when we arrived in the "Old Country", since we had all read about it and had been taught English literature and history in school. We also had had descriptions from relatives who'd been born there or had served overseas in World War I and, in many ways, England seemed just as we imagined it, although the countryside was more compact than Canadians were used to, and the distances much shorter. What did strike us in particular was how green everything looked – even in December. We were amazed, too, that every square foot of arable land was put to use and that every home had a vegetable "Victory Garden", as well as flowers growing in profusion.

Mona and Helen and I have a room on the third floor of our billet overlooking the sea, the strand and some beautiful gardens and lawns. Roses in December! We eat in a large mess-hall in a former hotel not far away. Good food, and well-cooked. It's cold weather, but no worse than our last week in the Dominion as far as cold feet go. We wear everything we own to bed. There's a fire in the grate on the ground floor and at night we heat water in our mess-tins to fill hot water bottles. We have fire-places in our rooms, but of course no fuel for them; also a wash-basin with cold and (occasionally) hot water. There isn't much wrong with the hot water facilities. It's just that by the time hot water hits a cold tub, there are great clouds of steam and in half a minute it's just another cold bath.

Every household and hotel in the U.K. was required by law to paint a four-inch line around the inside of their bathtubs in order to help conserve water supplies and discourage excess, but whatever the depth of the water, a hot bath was something to be relished whenever the opportunity presented itself.

We have resumed the old College argument of, "Who Is Going To Shut the Window in the Morning?" We have missed breakfast, to date, and have tea instead at ten a.m. My cough hangs on, but it is gradually fading. I feel extremely fit, otherwise, and the sea-voyage did Mona and me a lot of good, I am sure.

I need hardly dwell on the pride we have in being Canadian Airwomen serving in England, but it's probably not hard to tell that we think it's all right to be here. Our WAAF NCOs are dandies! We have found it a bit tricky understanding orders in a hurry, but we will soon be used to the accent. We march miles daily from building to building – mostly uphill! And we begin to perceive that in Canada we had it easy, for around here everyone seems to work to the utmost. Everybody seems to have enough to get by on – just. But there are few frills or luxuries. It's interesting to see the war-effort close up.

Dec. 12th, 1943

We've had a grand week, and Friday we were given a 36-hour-pass, so we all left at noon for London. After lining up for a cab, I was finally taken in tow by a couple of RCAMC officers who had been at the McGill Medical School. They set me down at the Daily Express Office in Fleet Street, where George's Aunt Olga works, and I met Olga there – our first meeting. We had tea in the office and then went by bus to the Strand Palace Hotel for dinner. Soup, and a very solid second course, then coffee and flan (something like pie, but what we call pie is a tart to the British).

After dinner, I rang up Grant Hollingworth in a nearby town. He is the husband of a friend of mine, Catherine, who at the present time is teaching in Ormstown. Grant is Padre at the Canadian Neurological Hospital Unit here. We arranged that I should stop off to see him on Saturday on my way back to camp.

I shall never forget the trip to Olga's in Streatham on the bus. There had been a blood-red moon early in the evening and by the time we started to Olga's, London town was bathed in moonlight. The Thames was silver, and Westminster and the Houses of Parliament looked like pictures in a fairy-tale book.

In the morning I accompanied Olga as far as her office and then

**Wartime London by moonlight...
National Gallery and St. Martin-in-the-Fields.**

Fox Photos ltd. London

71

set out for Canada House. The welcome there was warm and from there I was directed to the Canadian Girls' Club, just a block away.

There were several Canadian canteen-workers there and several of my pals had stayed there overnight. I had coffee with them (good coffee, too) and got directions about how to travel about in the neighbourhood. Canada House and the Club are both in the shadow of Nelson's monument in Trafalgar Square and I had only to cross the Square in front of the lions who guard the old boy to reach St. Martin-in-the-Fields. I went in search of the Verger and discussed the business of wedding Banns. He broke the news to me that either George or I has to be a resident of the parish for two weeks previous to the wedding. I won't know until the end of the week *when* I get leave.

From there I went to the Beaver Club and then to the Royal Bank in Cockspur Street where I was able to cash an English cheque, at last! More fun! All the time I was trotting around, I kept running across friends from Canada. And when I went back to the Club for lunch, I met some CWACs whom I knew. Then it was time to leave for Waterloo Station and I had my first glimpse of Waterloo Bridge by daylight. I caught the train with more than usual ease, thanks to many, many people.

Grant met my train at Basingstoke and we drove up to the Neurological Hospital. It is on an old estate which has been taken over by the Canadians. Great lawns and rolling meadows, hedges and shrubbery, and then – the mansion! Built of heavy stone, with a long drive leading up to it; it has huge pillars at the front door. The Hospital has been built onto the back and the main building serves as quarters for the staff. I was interested in the fifteen-foot ceilings, the huge open fire-places, the heavy curtains and the very solid shutters. There is carving over every door. Tea was served in a vast hall in which our voices seemed to echo. One of the Nursing Sisters took me under her wing and I left my knap-sack and respirator in her room. The bathroom adjoining was to scale, with a tub that I swear is ten by four!

We climbed all sorts of stair-cases and I rather expected to hear that we would presently meet a ghost, but no such luck! After tea Grant took me through the Hospital to see the equipment and the Operating Rooms. I have been through the Montreal Neurological Institute and this set-up compares favorably, if a layman can judge from the descriptions of instruments and methods. All the Sisters were trained at the M.N.I. and I feel very lucky to have had an opportunity to see the hospital here and under such pleasant circumstances. The Sisters were making up Christmas stockings for some of the evacuated children down in the village.

To escape the threat of bombing raids or the possible invasion of England by the Germans, a great many British children were sent as war-guests to families in Canada or the United States for the duration of the war. Others, whose families lived in and around London or on the south coast, were placed with families in rural areas within England. The trauma of this long separation was alleviated, at least in part, by the efforts of well-meaning Servicemen and women stationed in England, who attempted to bring a little happiness into the lives of these little ones whenever they could.

Grant is to play Santa on Saturday and the children are coming up to the hospital for a Christmas Tree party. Most of the candy and all the gifts and knitted things were sent by Canadians who had been patients of the Sisters when the latter were on private cases at home.

After our tour, Grant took me down to the village to an inn. We had a scotch and soda and then soup and pheasant. Good! The car came back for us at eight and I caught a train to Camp. In the hurry I left my gas-mask somewhere and may yet be on charge for not having it with me – but it was worth it!

I had had lunch with Grant's wife about a month ago, on the last Saturday I was in Montreal, so I was able to bring over comparatively recent news of her. He has been over here nearly three years. What a long time it is!

Mona is moving off, but Helen and I stay here, so our little trio is splitting up. There are no orders for us yet.

Since George and I had both received permission from our respective commanding officers to be married, we decided on January 22 and chose London as the most logical place, as the members of the wedding party would be coming from various postings all over England. We agreed on a centrally located church, and opted for a small reception after the ceremony, to be followed by a wedding trip to Cornwall. To comply with the "resident for two weeks" rule, George left a suitcase at the Charing Cross Hotel for the fortnight prior to the wedding.

As I had received permission from the Air Force to marry in January, it was deemed impractical to send me elsewhere until after the wedding. My posting to Digby in Lincolnshire was not made effective until early February. Meanwhile my WD companions drifted off, a few at a time, to their respective duties, while I remained with the WAAFs who were stationed permanently in Bournemouth. I had no duties, but was able to take my turn in the RAF/RCAF Post Office. The town was alive with RCAF airmen – both ground and flight-crews awaiting their postings; so there was plenty of companionship and time for excursions to movies and dances. In the mornings and afternoons we also found a variety of tea-rooms where we could indulge in tea and a bun.

This non-working time also afforded me an opportunity to familiarize myself with the intricacies of British money, the telephone system and the "drive on the left" traffic flow, as well as the chance to get to know the local shops and, from time to time, the inside of an air raid shelter.

Every city, town and hamlet had air raid shelters and "safe" quarters where people could take refuge. Although the majority of us had experienced Blackouts in Canada, we were unprepared for the real thing....air-raid sirens, ambulances, fire reels and the sound of anti-aircraft guns in the distance, with planes zooming overhead and unexplained flashes of light.

Have just been over with the gang collecting my weekly ration of chocolate – a quarter of a pound, in a bar. We are also allowed forty cigarettes without tax, it says here. After that they cost one and six for ten. The chocolate is Cadbury's and very good. Alternate weeks our ration is hard candy, so we really do very well. Coffee isn't rationed at all, but the tea is always much better, so we usually stick to that.

I expect to be seeing Mary Taunton one of these days. I am staying in my own work, by the way...

Dec. 15th, 1943

Helen and I are taking time off to spoil ourselves. Last night (Tuesday) we were told we could have a Pass until midnight Friday; so we packed our Kit, and got out! Went to a very nice hotel, had a hot bath and washed our wigs. By eight P.M. we were both in bed, having creamed our faces, taken our cough syrup, used our "drops" for colds, and put our hair up. It's heaven to be warm! We have a little electric thing on the floor that gives off heat as much as six inches distant. We were up at 8:30. Had a dandy breakfast at nine. Porridge, bacon and a fried tomato(!) – the first I've seen – and toast with marmalade and tea. All our colds need is a little care and we shall be restored once more. We are *all* coughing. It sounds like a chorus!

Life is a muddle. No one wants us. Every plan changes on the hour. Parades to the train station in the middle of the night, only to find that they don't need or expect us where we were to go. So we are "seizing the moment" and making as much fun as we can. Mona and Paddy left suddenly, so Helen and I will be without them on our return to camp.

It will be nice to be posted permanently. Our laundry is in a sad state and we are just living from day to day. They sent our baggage off one day and we were to follow the next, but the plans were changed and goodness knows where our things were deposited. Or whether we shall see them again!

Money here is worth far less than the rate of exchange would have us believe. A Pound Sterling will go about as far as a two-dollar bill. Everything is terribly expensive so we are lucky, in a way, to get no coupons, since we have enough to do to keep going without buying rationed things as well. Books, which are one of my weaknesses, are prohibitive in price. And everything printed since 1939 is bound in paper, of course. Local phone calls involve the use of two pennies and local postage is 2 1/2 d, so that one really needs a sack to carry one's coins!

Marching on city streets and toting bags about has wreaked havoc on our feet. As one army chap said to us the other evening, "The army makes shoes without support, and then if your feet fit them, they won't enlist you because you're flat-footed". I'm sure my right arch fell last week. It certainly feels like it! Even the Padre is suffering, though, so apparently feet are no respecter of persons!

There is nothing we need. We are well-fed, and have all the necessities. We eat better food, I fear, than the civilians, which makes us feel lucky but humble and most grateful. We must be careful not to waste a thing. Every plateful has to be finished. I think the WAAFs consider us Canadians very spoiled, which we have been. They put up with us, but they have done without so much and we are just beginning to realize what sacrifices the British have made. It makes one think a bit.

Dec. 18, 1943

I have just returned from a couple of days near George. I had to change trains en route and had an hour to wait, so I went over to the Salvation Army Hut for some tea. Met a Canadian there from the West, who had been overseas in the last War with Dad – the Winnipeg Grenadiers, 78th Battalion. The only other occupant of my carriage during the rest of the journey was a British Tommy just back from North Africa, Sicily and Italy. I found him delightful and most interesting.

I always have a dreadful time trying to get the right train. One can't cross the tracks as there are bridges and more bridges and I'm always on the wrong platform! There's a train every minute, and what a job to get the right one. But I did manage, with several kind people's help.

George was to meet me at a suburban station – the equivalent of Westmount or Montreal West. The train went right through, so I had to cope with the Blackout to get back to the other station! But all's well that ends well. We met, had dinner at my hotel and went dancing.

Thursday I amused myself in and about the town. Couldn't remember where I lived or even the name of the street, but a very kind "Bobby" led me to the hotel. I went to my first real Punch and Judy show in the afternoon and loved it. The owner showed me the dolls afterwards. The "Punch" has been in his family for nearly two hundred and fifty years. He has been on the road with it himself since 1901.

George came in the evening and we had dinner at a local inn and then joined some of the boys at one of their favourite dives.

We had tea together yesterday morning and then it was time for my train. It involved three changes to get back to my camp. More fun! But I had a bright new diamond to keep me interested and lots to think about. The date is set for January 22nd, in St. Martin's, London – if it can be arranged – which George thinks it can. Dick O'Hagan, who is in the Forestry Corps, says he'll give the bride away if Chris doesn't get here in time. He's an old friend from home. So, five weeks from today, and then probably to Cornwall or Devon for a week. It looks from here as though it will be our only week together, since we get Leave only every three months and George doesn't expect to be around the next time.

The hotel where I stayed was filled with old folk. I do feel sorry for the old people. They find the cold so hard on them. An old chap of 84 came over and chatted. He was Commandant of R.M.C. from '09 to '13, or so. Doesn't know anyone less than a Brigadier and was quite upset that I didn't recognize his friends' names. But they're all of my grandparents' generation. I wish he had put on his uniform. I'd like a squint at his medals! So one meets all kinds, from the ranks of the 78th Battalion and the British Tommy from Italy, to the octogenarian who left Sandhurst in 1879! Another old dear there at the hotel has five grandsons on Active Service. Lady Knight, the widow of a land-holder in Hampshire, lives there. She has been bombed out twice and now has no home. The war is a leveller, is it not?

It is difficult to imagine what it must have been like to leave your home in the morning, not knowing whether by the time you got back that evening you'd find yourself without a roof over your head. Or to arrive at the train station only to discover that your rail line to suburban London had been eliminated by enemy bombers. How did these people manage to carry on day after day, month after month, for years on end, hearing the sirens, heading off to the air-raid shelters and emerging to view devastation on all sides? Even fifty years after the fact, I am still filled with admiration and wonder at the ability of the British people to withstand and carry on.

Came back to find nobody home and the door wide open – literally. It turned out that the remaining few had been moved to another billet, so I followed. Helen had come back from her trip in the middle of the night and had had a hard time finding her way to the new place.

It's nearly five weeks now since I left Montreal with a stack of clean shirts and collars. They won't let us send anything to the laundry here "in case it doesn't get back in time". In time for what, you ask? Ah, that is a ten-dollar question and there is no answer. It's similar to "Why is a raven like a writing-desk?" And there are other things, too, which remind me of Alice and the Mad Hatter! Neither may we have Leave (for the same reason – we might not get back in time!) but we are faring well on the odd "48".

Meantime I am learning to turn my collars inside out after a couple of days and have lost any taboos I once had about wearing an unironed shirt. Our baggage is still at the cross-roads at Waterloo Station.

The flour here is all of one kind – made of barley, I think; so that bread, buns, puddings, Yorkshire pudding and pies all have the same flavour. It's very marked at first, but one quickly grows used to it. We don't have any butter – it's all margarine of course, and the only milk is in tea or coffee. There is no difference, as far as I can tell, in the taste of margarine and butter, but both are rationed. Meals in hotels and restaurants are restricted to three courses, with tea or coffee extra. The maximum price is 5 shillings for the three courses, but in most places there is what they call a "Service Charge" and drinks and coffee are to be had at a price, so that the bill soon mounts – in spite of the five shilling maximum.

I hope now that we don't move before Christmas. We've made friends; know all the Canteen folk and the boys here are being good to us, too. Helen and I have an invitation to a civilian household for Christmas Day, so I hope we can accept. There are dozens of places to go dancing, a pub on every corner and plenty of movies. I have been sticking close, with Mona and Helen, to three lads who came over on the boat with us, but now that Mona has gone, our little party bids fair to being broken up. It's never quite the same when the girls go to other Stations. Paddy has left too. Since we have had no work as yet, there is nothing to be gained by resting and we spend every night down in the town until about ten. Places close up after that.

One would expect that any dogs to be found in England would have to be of use to justify their feeding, but there are a large number of lap-dogs – Pekes, and their lesser friends of flea-size. Of the larger breeds, one rarely sees a mongrel and never a stray. Watch-dogs and rat-killers are valuable, of course. There is provision made for animals in the air-raid shelters.

In one old, disused shelter which we passed on the train yesterday there was a goat standing in the door-way – just as though he were the lord of his castle.

Dec. 19, 1943

Sunday has passed without incident – almost. Helen and I have been moved into yet newer, or shall I say *stranger* billets. We're in a room now with four WAAFs. Their accents are all thick, each different from the others and we can't understand a word they say. Helen, more accustomed to the various tongues than I am, tells me that they swear quite a lot, but it's all beyond me.

We are without chairs, cupboards or hooks, so our belongings have to be stowed away in our knap-sacks. Since I am prone to strew my stuff over any given area, I find myself restricted considerably.

Last night was a good one for sleeping. No air-raids. The first thing I knew, it was 9:30 and we had slept through Parade. The other WDs are billeted elsewhere, so we are a little Dominion of our own, Helen and I. Deciding that, for today at least, "we'd had it" – (a phrase used to describe something which has come and gone), I went back to sleep. Woke up in time for coffee and then Helen and I went to St. Peter's Church. It's the same one that George and I went to two weeks ago when he was here – the Mother Church in the city. Very ornate. The Banns were called. The Vicar of St. Alban's preached the sermon.

Helen and I slept away the early part of the afternoon and then Helen went off for tea to some British friends and I to some others – relatives of Auntie Dot's. Great stories about their family dog. He is a greyhound called Wallace. It seems that at one time he was sent away to train with other dogs in Aerodrome Protection, but after nine weeks he was sent home with a very polite letter. "We are sorry, but your dog has had to be discharged. He is a confirmed rabbit-hunter". Apparently he guarded the 'drome faithfully until a cotton-tail appeared, at which point he whipped off in pursuit. Wallace doesn't care about chickens, but he has cost his owners Pounds for the ducks he has killed.

I had supper with Andy Sharp, a Pilot Officer from Saskatchewan – one of the boys I met on the boat coming over. He used to show sheep at fairs out west and won a sheep-shearing contest or two. He's extremely good to me and we have fun together. He says he's coming to the wedding. I hope he can get the time off.

We are wondering what it will be like to be here for Christmas, and betting on whether there will be turkey in the Mess, or not.

There are still roses in the gardens. I saw some today, but I can't figure out why the things are still blooming – I wouldn't be! And roses in gardens don't make it seem like Christmas. Our new billets are practically on the beach and if there's one thing that makes me want to go back to bed in the morning, it's the sight of great grey waves and white breakers rolling in on the sand. Brr!

I am writing to you in the Knights of Columbus Hostel – the only place where I can find a fire to put my feet in. There was a party here last night and we all came to it. Peanut butter sandwiches and Cokes are reserved for the Canadians in all the Canteens. The English on the whole won't go near either of them, so we do the rest!

This is an easy life – no work, so far, but we would like to get cracking. There will come a day, I suppose, when we'll wish we could skip Parade without fear of being put on the hook for it, but just at the moment we are feeling a little browned off from idleness. And we do miss Mona and Paddy.

Dec. 21st, 1943

Helen and I took a jaunt by bus down to Christchurch for the afternoon. Shelley's Memorial was among the many interesting things to be seen. Am now steeped in architecture, poetry, and more beauty than I can bear in one day!

Part of the Christchurch Priory dates back to 1066 and all that. Before Old Henry VIII did away with Priories, only the monks were allowed into the inner part. The general townspeople worshipped in an outer part and they never saw this section.

To continue about the Christchurch Priory. We had heard the legend about it and were anxious to see the Church for ourselves. A fifteen-minute bus-ride found us in the High Street of the town. The story goes that when the original priory, which still stands, was being built just after 1066, one of the beams was too short. The workmen left (presumably when the five o'clock whistle blew) and on their return the next morning the beam which had been faulty was the same length as all the others. Their conclusion was that only the Master Carpenter could have performed such a miracle. The beam is still to be seen.

The architecture is superb. The Choir Screen was added to the Priory late in the 14th Century, and the Lady Chapel in 1395, when it was fashionable to erect altars to the Virgin. The Priory proper was opened to the townsfolk in Henry VIII's time.

I was interested in the development of the church windows. The early Norman windows supplied little light, so larger ones were made. First on the north side, since that was the darkest and later, opposite, they built larger ones with an experiment – the little circle at the top – I don't know what it's called – which provided more light still, and was a little more ornate.

One of the memorials is that of a Knight who died in the Wars of the Roses and his Lady. Life-size images of the two lie hand-in-hand – the Knight with his feet on his little dog and the Lady's head-dress very much a thing of the times.

Some of the oldest epitaphs are on the great stone slabs that make the floor. They are worn, now, but legible in places. The more recent 17th and 18th century and even the 19th century tablets bear very flowery phrases.

There are entire walls devoted to the memory of families of soldiers killed out in India, Egypt and the Crimea. The Cameron men, for instance, who must have been the backbone of the Cameron Highlanders. A few are to the memory of men killed in the last War and one or two in this one. A spot commemorates England's sons in war from the 11th Century to this one. The hallowedness of the place was not lost on either of us!

Then there was all the heavy oak carving, the old Norman Tower, the crypt, and Shelley's memorial.

Monday night we went to see *Fired Wife* with Diana Barrymore, and it was very good. The other so-called "attraction" was a miserable Gestapo thing, *The Strange Death of Adolf Hitler*. I beg of you not under any circumstances to sit through it. I don't know why I sat through it, except that I was too scared to move! Gruesome is too mild a word.

Yesterday afternoon Helen and I saw Jeannette McDonald and Nelson Eddy in *New Moon*. It's very old, but wears well, and I enjoyed it. In the evening we went with the lads to a pub, and then on to dinner.

I was about to say that this leaves me high and dry. But we are neither high nor dry! We are in yet different billets. This time our room has not even a view to commend it. It's a cosy little spot in the cellar! When it rains the gutters overflow just behind our beds, and the dear old English windows won't budge, so we can't shut them! Our kit is on the mantel-shelf, so that it absorbs less moisture than if it were on the floor. We rock with laughter every night when we retire into our dungeon. It's too ridiculous for words. Wonderful what one can get used to! The plutocrats upstairs may have a bit more comfort, but they don't have any more fun than we do! We are lucky to have shelter at all, and we fully realize it.

Our lounge and Mess are looking very festive with holly, streamers of coloured paper and chains, great red bows, and evergreen branches. We have been whiling away the time helping to decorate. I've never seen holly growing before, but this came from a nearby garden. We are having a Christmas party on the night of the 25th. I've asked Andy Sharp, who has been so good to me. I'd be lost without him.

I have now accomplished the art of jumping off a moving bus. But I think I won't try it too often. I've only seven lives left – (I lost one between Canada and here, carrying *baggage*)

I shall never, never be able to learn English table manners! The uses of knife, fork and spoon baffle me. The Englishman hangs onto his knife for dear life all through the main course, and eats his dessert with both a spoon and a fork. Fine thing! When in Rome, I suppose one must do as the Romans do, but I find it very awkward!

We receive a Canadian paper printed in London for the Forces, containing a digest of the week's news. And we are becoming accustomed to English (war-time) cigarettes. The first one nearly ruins one's tongue, but it's a matter of habit. The chocolate and toffees are limited but of excellent quality. We saw oranges today in a store. These are reserved for children under five, which seems reasonable.

We shall no doubt make up for our idleness when we get to our jobs, but in the meantime our consciences are smitten. HQ, London, hasn't recovered yet from its surprise when we turned up. They have hidden their surprise admirably, though. No one would suspect that they knew we were here – judging from the attention we have not received! I wonder what sort of thing I'll be doing. So far I don't feel that I've justified the money spent on sending us here, since as yet no work has appeared to get our teeth into. Can one blame the boys who go a bit wild, when they have months of this idleness to put in?

Dec. 24, 1943

It's five o'clock, Eastern Daylight Time. Ten o'clock over here and Christmas Eve! Andy and I walked out along the cliffs this afternoon in the sunshine, admired the semi-tropical foliage and sat for an hour watching the waves come in over the sand. It's hard to realize that this is the twenty-fourth of December and that the shortest day of this year has come and gone.

We had tea in a tea-room near the beach. There were two young Englishmen at our table. The orchestra played a number of familiar pieces and then started on "A White Christmas". One chap remarked to the other, "Lovely tune, that, – but aren't the words slushy? ". It was all Andy and I needed! We both leapt to the attack and I'm sure the poor man thought us quite out of our minds. He took us more seriously than we had intended and apologized profusely for hurting our feelings; at which point we all laughed and went on to talk about other things – chiefly the differences between Canada and the U.K. as we see them. We agreed that the Blackout is "quite a game". Andy was rubbing an ankle which he had nearly broken last night in the dark! (We are just hearing by radio the Carillon in Ottawa play "O Canada". Did someone say "Music to my ears" ?)

For lack of anything better to do, Andy and I went to see another movie – my third this week and more than I usually see in half a year, but it passes the time. Tonight we saw Anna Neagle in *Yellow Canary*.

Shall be going to church in the morning, dinner in the Mess and to tea at the home of some civilian friends. I was going to go to the WAAF/RAF Party with Andy, but they needed a Duty N.C.O. for tomorrow night, so I've volunteered. No one particularly wants the job for Christmas Night. It lasts from 6 P.M. until 8.00 the next morning. Have to watch out for little incendiaries, and tuck in the WDs, newly arrived, in another hostel.

Helen is away on leave and Mona and Paddy have gone to greener fields, leaving me to the palatial room which is ours, and I do miss the crowd. So ends the carillon program, and this WD's first Christmas Eve in England.

Dec. 26th, 1943

Christmas has come and gone. A very merry one, here. We were entirely moved by the efforts of all to make it pleasant for us. We could not have had more kindness shown to us. The myth that the American troops can't live without the trifles to which they are accustomed at home seems to have been recounted about the Canadians as well. Everything was done to ensure that we would feel at home – short of a snowfall!

Christmas Day was beautiful in the balmy south. Sunshine, sea-breezes, white waves on a warm strand and all the comforts of a south sea island. Much, I imagine, as a December day might be in Victoria, B.C.

Rumour had it that for all good little soldier-girls and boys who made the effort to get up for breakfast Christmas morning, Santa was to bring a real egg. And he did, too! Poached, on toast. – And fresh milk on the cereal, as well.

The R.C.A.F. Band played in the great dining hall as we all filed in for dinner. Cream of tomato soup, turkey, baked potatoes, cauliflower, cabbage, dressing and lots of gravy. For dessert, Pudding with sauce – and wonderful mince pies. Coca-cola at each place and lots of beer. Christmas is the one day in the year when the Officers traditionally wait on the Ranks, so it was rather fun to have a Group-Captain (the C.O.) with the famous "scrambled eggs" (gold braid) on his hat, trotting around replenishing our mugs. The Air Crew – Sergeants, mostly – took great delight in calling out "Boy – more beer here, please!" And I rather think the Old Man enjoyed himself quite as much as we did. He had at least one sample from each mug as he poured, and he was rather a happy fellow at the end of the meal!

The little choir boys came around on Christmas Eve and sang Carols for their pennies. Today the church choirs had processions to various hostels and to the Hospital, wearing their surplices, and singing with great fervour.

At supper-time there appeared some Christmas cake and chocolate-coated biscuits. The pastry chefs had a regular art-exhibit of the cakes before we cut into them. One was three and a half feet long, with writing on it in pink frosting, and there were several smaller cakes (only two feet square!) with the names of the various sections on them – R.C.A.F., R.A.F., W.A.A.F. and WD

The beverages flowed freely. It's the one day in the year, apparently, when no one says a word to the drunken airman or the tipsy WAAF. And there were many of both.

I had tea at our civilian friends' in the afternoon – by a blazing fire! Ah me, altogether it was a Christmas Day we shall not forget.

Today comes the news in the papers that the Allies are nearing their objective towards the much-talked of Second Front. Roosevelt's choice of Eisenhower as Commander has been widely acclaimed by the English press and there is a great cheer going up at the thought of the possibilities of peace which surely will follow the Victory. And perhaps the coming year will see it all over and done with.

The general feeling is one of optimism, even though the casualties will of necessity be numerous. People here seem to think that that is inevitable and so is a European invasion. It's something of a relief to feel that perhaps this is their last winter of the depressing Black-out, and that next December may well see "The lights go on again".

It is no panic-stricken mob-view, this. The British, as far as I can see, are not habitually optimistic to the point of looking ahead too far, even if they are notably a cheerful crowd. Instead of the "let-down" feeling which so often follows Christmas celebration, there is an exhilaration which is simply amazing.

Hope is a pretty wonderful thing. One has only to let one's mind wander and ponder what it will mean to countries like France, Poland, Austria, Italy to be completely free of the Nazi heel. All we want is to see one family brought together, one father or son restored to his people, one couple glorying in a reunion, and then we will feel that it is time to go home. So far I have had no opportunity given to me to help in the task, but there will be ample to do – there is ample to do now, but we haven't been told yet where we begin.

We were amused by the British film, *Yellow Canary*, which we saw on Christmas Eve. It's thoroughly good in plot, but at one point a whole crowd of

Nazi spies and British Intelligence people end up in Halifax, N.S., and the hotel as shown on the screen is unlike anything Halifax ever had – "The Barrington Arms".

Of all my Christmas presents, guess which one I enjoyed most ? A round, red *apple*! We each got one, and it probably meant more to us Canadians than it would to the "natives". Three of us looked at our apples for hours – and only ate 'em just now!

At last they have admitted that this is the coldest winter this part of England has had in 20 years. We heard Roosevelt on Christmas Eve, and the King yesterday. We are listening just now to a service broadcast by the Archbishop of Canterbury from his study.

Four weeks from yesterday George and I shall be married. It seems a long time away but I suppose it really isn't!

Dec. 31st, 1943

The Old Year is dying and the New Year brings us the promise that our trip to England is to be justified – finally. We haven't been bored this last month – far from it! But our consciences pricked, as I never thought mine would, at the lack of a job. The R.C.A.F. has muddled through. For awhile it forgot about us and busied itself with that material of crimson hue which we know as red tape. But now – now it thinks that perhaps we *are* trained for a task – so to that task we go, before very long.

Mother seemed confident in a recent letter that Chris would be here in time to give me away. It' ll be great, if he does come.

I landed in Sick Bay, R.A.F. for a couple of days with "flu". It's not an experience I'd have missed for anything. I've seen a lot of interesting things and this place is one of Disraeli's former homes – vast halls, great windows, high ceilings, panelling and all the rest.

One of the WAAF Officers brought me a little grey kitten for company. I call her "Phyllis", and she sleeps at the foot of my bed. I've grown very attached to her, but shall have to leave her behind, I'm afraid. Kittens don't travel well in dunnage bags.

While in Bournemouth I spent a couple of days in the Air Force Hospital with nothing more serious than a sinus cold. The day the WAAF medical officer was discharging me, I asked if I might have a word with her, explaining that marriage was imminent and that my Canadian doctor had given me the name of a birth-control product. The Boys were all issued condoms as a matter of course, but no such provision had been made for Servicewomen.

The WAAF M.O. invited me into her office and ascertained that the two doors were both firmly closed behind us before informing me in hushed tones that this kind of information was not being made available to WAAF personnel. Would I perhaps like a book to read? I thanked her, but decided not to accept. Evidently I had made a sensible choice since soon afterwards, in passing the window of the local chemist's (drug store), I observed that it was piled high with a variety of birth-control products.

I quite shocked the W.A.A.F. Medical Officer by discussing contraceptives with her. They don't believe in giving this kind of advice to the Airwomen here, as I might have guessed from the appalling number of girls, both married and unmarried, who are in the Air Force Hospital waiting to be discharged from the Service. Instead, I was offered a book to read – which I declined, with thanks. The M.O. thinks me "a very unusual type". I was sorry to have embarrassed her.

Our WAAF Corporal has a heart as big as all outdoors and we're going to miss her when we go. That's the damnable part of the Service. You just get settled and make friends and then off you go! Or else they go and it's like a kaleidoscope – the patterns are lovely, but no two are the same and you can't recapture a pattern once it has departed.

We wondered, when we left Nova Scotia, just how many of the girls we had known for six or seven months would turn up again later. I remember watching a bus-load of girls pull out from Rockcliffe to go to the train, the night our Basic Training was completed and we had graduated. I was feeling just a bit sick at the sight of the crowd leaving, and my cousin, Mary Taunton, who was then my O.C., came up behind me and said, "You wish *you* were posted, don't you, Hawkins?" I forget what I said, but her reply was "Oh, well, – cheer up – there'll be a posting for you, too, some day". And as it turned out, Mary and I and the red-headed WD Sergeant who was our Squadron's instructor during Basic, have appeared on consecutive posting lists, in that order, and are all in England now!

So one never can tell, I suppose, what is in store. The red-headed Sergeant I mentioned had been out in Vancouver almost ever since last February, when she put the fear of the RCAF into us. Even now I tremble when I think of her, though now that I have been in the Old Country two weeks longer than she, I can feel quite patronising – at times!

The Hospital Attendants are a good sort. They entertain by the half-hour – when they have time – with accounts of the Battle of Britain. I am spell-bound by some of the things I hear. No wonder they think their twelve-hour duty nowadays is a breeze. They admit, though, quite readily, that they are tired – not only because of their work, but by the restrictions imposed by the Blackout, the rations, the lack of luxury – or even comfort – and the worry they've had for over four years.

Every one of them has had a tragedy, it seems. One girl is the sole survivor of a family of seven. Her parents and some of the rest of the family were lost in raids; her brothers have been killed in action or are "Missing at Sea." The story is one that can be repeated by each and all – to a greater or a lesser extent. One of my favourite Attendants is a girl whose husband is in the Royal Navy. The last she heard from him was a letter promising that he would be home for Christmas. She's a plucky sort. I do hope she hears from him soon.

I have a wireless [radio] in my room and there is central heating, so it's what the English call "not bad". Helen came in this afternoon to tell me all about her week's Leave. It sounded all right, too.

Jan. 2, 1944

The marriage date approaches! Eleven o'clock, three weeks from yesterday, definitely at St.Martin-in-the-Fields. Have just been talking to the prospective groom. Everything is going very smoothly and we have reason to believe that Chris will come. The Banns are completed and George says he has neither given the wedding-ring to anyone else, nor lost it! We are going down to St. Ives afterwards.

Before George went up to London to arrange for our marriage, he asked some of his fellow officers whether they could recommend a suitable place for a reception after the wedding. He received several suggestions and after he had made all the necessary arrangements at St.Martin-in-the-Fields, he decided to look around for a suitable venue in the vicinity. He was unimpressed with the exteriors of the places he'd been referred to earlier; however, as he walked along he came upon the name "Claridge's" written on the sidewalk. On closer inspection he concluded that this place looked a cut above the others and went into to make further inquiries. The staff were more than helpful and quoted him a modest price for the reception – one pound per head.

As we were due to leave for Cornwall early the following day, they suggested that the hotel's Bridal Suite would be available for our use. Once again the charge was comparatively modest, so everything was arranged accordingly. When George returned to the Battalion and reported the results of his successful foray, his friends were astounded to learn that this green young Canadian officer had managed to arrange a wedding reception at one of London's foremost hotels, whose guest list included the names of many of Europe's crowned heads.

We "Innocents Abroad" later learned from British friends that several of the places George had spurned en route to Claridge's because of their shabby exteriors were frequented by Churchill.

My RCAF (WD) friends have left me here. Meanwhile, being a Parade of One, I am attaching myself to the WAAF and have a job sorting mail in the Post Office. It's interesting work and the Postal Staff are a merry gang. I would have gone off my head had I not found this to do and they seem satisfied to have an extra hand.

Jan. 6th, 1944

Went shopping to buy an Air Force shirt and an Air Force scarf. It has just appeared in orders that we may wear the latter. Since there is a rule about not turning up one's coat collar unless the Commanding Officer permits it in Daily Orders, one just freezes until he decides he'd like to turn his own up!

Andy Sharp and I started out in search of tea after the movie last night, but the short period of quiet that we have been enjoying was once more interrupted by sirens, so we didn't wander far. However, a little later there came the very familiar sound of our own bombers overhead – heading off to do their little job on the Continent.

> *When the sirens went off, every home and office had a shelter where people could take cover until the "All Clear" was sounded. These shelters were not necessarily bomb-proof, but provided at least a degree of protection from falling shrapnel or beams and masonry. Supplies of food and water were also stored in the shelters as a precautionary measure. In London, hundreds of families moved into the Tube stations of the underground railway to spend the night, exchanging privacy and comfort for greater security below ground level.*

Saturday afternoon a WAAF Corporal, Pat Forbes, took our Sergeant and me out to her home in Swanage by train. We had tea in a little tea-shop and then walked out a mile or so to the Corporal's house. It turned out that the Corporal is an <u>artist</u>. Has designed costumes for a couple of good companies in London, as well as the Ballet – is terribly keen on the stage and knows a lot. I sat in a trance while she and the Sergeant talked about stars of the London stage, performances they'd seen, and places they'd been to in town in peace-time. All like fairy tales to me. It was a side of the Corporal that I hadn't known existed. How little one knows of one's friends, sometimes.

One of the WAAF Sergeants has just come back from Lincolnshire, and says the girls are living in "cottages" that used to be the Warrant Officers' married quarters in peace time. Better than we had hoped for, and Helen is saving me a bed, so it looks promising. She writes that there is a fire in every room and that we are to share a room. Very good!

Wing Officer K. Walker's office is very near to St. Martin's, and the impression conveyed was that if she were interested in attending our wedding and had the time, we would be honoured, delighted, etc. It was awfully good of the WAAF Officer to write. She seemed to think it was the thing to do; so perhaps Wing Officer Walker will turn up – or, more likely, send a deputy to be witness to the fact. Had an interview with her when we first came, and then later George and I ran into her on the station platform while waiting for George's train.

January 17/1/44

Tonight saw a very good movie *Sun Valley Serenade* with Sonja Henie in it. Plenty of skating, lots of skiing and more than enough of Tyrone Power, who holds little charm for me. A year ago I was at Piedmont at the Winsum Inn, falling around the hills, which compare favourably with anything Hollywood can offer in an imitation of Switzerland.

The only thing that gets me up at all these mornings is the threatened inspection by the C.O. I lie for half an hour wondering what I'll say if the door opens and he and his entourage come in; how I'll explain away the fact that I am still in bed. Never can think of a reasonable reason, so up I get – just in case. After a spot o'tea with the WAAF I'm off to the Post Office, where I re-address a dozen or so letters, have lunch with Pat Forbes at the Mess, then work in her office in the afternoon, sharpening pencils. Tea at four, supper at five, collect the afternoon mail, write a letter or two, then trot off to a pub or a movie with the crowd. Have given up worrying about not earning my keep. Found that no one else was giving it a second thought.

With only a matter of days left before the wedding, time for writing letters was limited. In the end, my next letter to Marion Strang was written from Cornwall during our honeymoon, to bring her up to date on how everything had gone. A chance meeting with one of the guests at the Tregenna Castle Hotel also provided me with information I felt would be of particular interest to her.

Mary Buch with her matron-of-honour, Mona (Langley) Murdock, St. Martin-in-the-Fields, London, January 22, 1944.

Tregenna Castle Hotel,
Ives, Cornwall.
January 28, 1944.

Friday afternoon three of the WAAF N.C.O.s and I travelled up to London and George, Mona and Mona's brother, Ellis Langley, (R.C.A.F. – just back from a tour of Ops. in the Middle East) met us at the station. Mona had booked a double room for herself and me at the Dorchester, so we went there first and sampled some very smooth brandy that Ellis had brought from Algeria. Then George phoned Tommy Havill, the Best Man, at the Mount Royal and he said that my brother, Chris, had not arrived yet, but to come on over anyway.

Mona preceded me into Tommy's room and I followed, to find Chris hiding behind a door, smoking his pipe and wearing a silly grin. I flew into his arms and burst into floods of happy tears. Then Tommy began handing around Scotches and we talked a blue streak before going down to dinner.

Olga Buch (George's aunt) had invited us out to Streatham for the evening, but the flack from Ack-Ack guns was too heavy and the taxi-driver turned around half-way there. So we all went back to Tommy's room for another hour or so.

A total of 268 tons of bombs fell on London that night. We were later told that it was the worst onslaught since the Blitz of 1940, and marked the beginning of what became known as "the Little Blitz". Small wonder that our taxi driver was not overjoyed to have us five rollicking Canadians as passengers. Being already well-primed by generous drams of whiskey – as we crossed London that night, the War was not uppermost in our minds. We laughed and joked, amidst blaring sirens and people running for cover. The sky was lit up and the noise deafening, but we remained more or less oblivious until the cab driver opened his little window and announced gruffly that he wasn't prepared to take us any further and would be turning back. We could either return to central London with him or get out and be left to our own devices. Since we were in unknown territory in the middle of a blackout, we quickly elected to stick with our driver and return to Tommy's hotel room.

Unfortunately Aunt Olga had no telephone, so we were unable to call and explain our absence, but assumed she would have heard about the raid and understood. As it turned out she had no idea why we had failed to arrive and imagined that we'd simply found more interesting ways to amuse ourselves. All subsequent attempts at explanation fell on deaf ears and Aunt Olga's initial blessing of the marriage of her nephew and his bride was withdrawn until further notice.

In true English style, that night Mona and I left our shoes outside the door and the next morning we found them beautifully polished. The valet came up at eight a.m. and took our uniforms away. Brought them back pressed to a turn and the buttons gleaming. For the first time since I've been in the Air Force, I broke down and wore grey *silk* stockings. Don't as a rule approve of them, but this was an occasion!

We put on our best collars and ties and really felt quite swish. When we went down to breakfast, Helen Woodcroft joined us and Ellis turned up too. They all insisted that I had to eat porridge, which I obediently did. Afterwards we all went back to the room again

St. Martin-in-the-Fields Church, London.

and Mona did my nails while Helen combed out my hair and Ellis poured brandy. They insisted it was the thing to do so (once more obedient) I swallowed a bit, while Ellis took three or four swigs, saying that he'd already been through his own wedding and knew what an ordeal it was.

Then, armed with our prayer books (Mona and I), we all went down to the lobby and the battle of the taxis began. Our car finally did arrive for us, but not before Ellis had told the entire hotel that a car had been ordered and it was *urgent*. I'm sure from all the commotion, that the bystanders thought one of us was on the way to a hospital instead of a church. Ellis and Helen smoked furiously on the trip to St. Martin's and kept asking me how I felt.

Chris met us at the door with the Verger and the Curate, Mr. Oswald. As we went up the aisle I caught a glimpse of several faces. We think there were

Newlyweds George and Mary Buch outside St. Martin-in-the-Fields, London, January 22,1944.

about fifty people altogether – many of whom we hadn't seen for months or even years. Wing Officer Walker did come – with an Aide – and this was much appreciated.

The Service went without a hitch. I looked sideways at the boys. Tommy's face was a study; however he produced the ring at the proper moment, in spite of being full of scotch. When George and I came to our lines, the Minister said nothing about "obey", nor did George "endow" me with all his wordly goods, but promised to "share" them with me, which is much better.

The trip down to Cornwall was long and tiring. We managed to get some sandwiches at Exeter, but were mighty hungry by nine p.m. when we arrived. They had a good dinner waiting, fortunately.

St. Ives' is quite, quite beyond description. The village itself is not unlike Lower Town Quebec City. Streets wide enough for exactly one bus and sidewalks twelve inches wide. (We measured them.) The Castle is on a hill and our room looks out to the west and the sea. The beach is beautiful and between here and the village there is a fairy-land of hedges, woods and little brooks. The golf-course is well-kept, and everything is so *green*. We went down to Penzance by bus one day this week – a thoroughly enjoyable jaunt.

The Tregenna Castle Hotel is luxurious and the food excellent. There are a few Canadians here – Betty Osler of Montreal, whose husband, Campbell Osler is with the Canadians in Italy. Two nights ago when we were having coffee, a Canadian captain came over and asked if we would join him and his wife. We introduced ourselves and when the Captain's wife said, "I'm Alice Sorby", I remarked that she sounded Canadian. She said she was and did I not know her name? Turned out that she is Officer Commanding of all CWAC in the U.K. She and her husband are from Winnipeg and she was on the first CWAC course at Macdonald in February, '42. She and Wing Officer Walker hold the same position in the respective Services, so I would judge that Mrs. Sorby is a Major or a Lieut-Colonel. She has just won the M.B.E.

We are leaving here tomorrow and shall strike out for Bournemouth. George has fourteen days; I only have nine and must report Monday morning. I expect to be starting for Lincolnshire early in the week. They were phoning before I left to find out why I hadn't turned up for work. Wish now that they'd write and say, "The war is over – you needn't come back!" If I go north early enough, George and I will be able to travel as far as London together. If not, then I shall stay with him at his hotel and just put in an appearance at the Admin. office whenever they require it – twice a day, likely.

There is one thing about which I would like to devote an entire letter to you. I had a long conversation with a man here, who was in Hong Kong as late as three days after it fell. Perhaps you have talked to someone from there. I don't know. This chap is not young. He escaped the Japanese twice – once at Hong Kong and once in China. He is a European, wears the uniform of his country and is now employed by the British Government. I must tell you what he had to say.

For one thing, he believes what we all had heard; that the first frenzy after capturing a town is the worst. He said that as soon as the Japanese Regular Army arrived in Hong Kong they settled down to putting things in order. He saw the atrocities at the beginning, but he says that his experience of Japanese camps makes him certain that nothing like that would continue, once the first mad lust for booty was appeased. I asked him as many questions as came to mind and he patiently answered them.

He said that Hong Kong itself was a luxurious spot and that even by the time he left, they were putting the reservoirs and water-systems etc. back into use and that it is quite likely that in no time at all the men would have hot water – depending of course on the situation of the various camps. Food was a grim question in the beginning, but he said that the last news he had before he left China was that the Japanese were coming round to giving the boys more than just rice. He said that bribery would get one a long way – that the boys get a ration of cigarettes and that he had had drinking water while he was there. He said they wouldn't suffer from cold, but that at times the heat was very oppressive.

Another thing that interested me was the recreation. He said that in the camp he was in, they used to have sports and races – rugby and so on – and they competed for such prizes as a hand-carved wooden drinking cup or an extra ration of cigarettes.

He was definitely an agent – this fellow – so he came in for a fair share of interrogation. He said, however, that the Canadian boys would not be subjected to the third degree, unless they had any success at all in trying to escape; in which case the Japs pumped them to find out who, of their own men, were traitors, giving aid. Camp life varied little from that in any other military situation and since there were many English and Canadian men together, he thinks they would maintain good standards of cheerfulness.

It was hard to believe that I was actually conversing with someone who had been out there in December of 1941. Talking to him, Hong Kong seemed less remote and "out of this world" than it had before. The Captain said that *nothing* was as bad as it had seemed to us in North America and he left me with the remark, "Your Canadian will not suffer".

This information, at the time, may have been comforting, however, we now know that the Canadians interned by the Japanese did, indeed, suffer a great deal.

PART FIVE

Lincolnshire Posting
February – March 1944

Lincolnshire
Feb. 4th, 1944

Thursday (yesterday) I was at the train station at half-past seven to get my train north to Lincolnshire. I had loads of baggage plus my instructions. Got to Waterloo Station around 11:00 and the Railway Transport Office got me a WAAF and a truck to take me to King's Cross. I had half an hour there, so I snatched a mug of tea and a bun at the Salvation Army Hut. A Canadian soldier was going my way and helped me put my kit in the van and get a seat.

We had to change at Grantham and the train was late, so we missed our connection to the next place. We had two hours to wait there; had tea and at seven o'clock I started off again. Had another change before I got a bus to where I am now. It was after nine o'clock when I arrived and I don't think I shall ever be reluctant to go *anywhere*, having just crossed England. You can't imagine what it's like trying to cope, and by the time darkness descends, one simply gropes in the dark. What a picnic!

Helen had everything ready for me – sheets, blankets, toast and tea – and we talked until she had to go to work at midnight. I spent today getting documented and making polite explanations about my baggage, which is along the line

LAW Helen Woodcroft and Mary Buch with kitbag outside billets at RCAF Station, Digby, Lincolnshire, February 1944.

93

where I got the bus. Shall write a sequel some day to that series of E.V. Lucas – "In Search of Baggage".

The house in which we live is one of a row which, in pre-war days, were the Warrant Officers' married quarters. Helen and I live in one of the two upstairs rooms. There is a kitchen as well as one other room below, and we can cook there over the fire in the grate. The food here is grim, so we shall be making it go farther by what we can swipe from the Mess – bread and marge and jam. We have some tea and powdered milk and I can see that we are to spend much of our time keeping the fire going.

This is the land of windmills. Just when I was getting used to the climate of the south coast, I had to come up to the windy north. However, it is most invigorating. The Salvation Army has supplied each of us with a hand-knitted scarf and mitts and heavy socks and they are much appreciated!

A bus takes us out to where we work. My shift has been on Graveyard for nearly a fortnight, so we shall be working days after about the 8th. We have a day off during the change-over to the other shift and Helen and I are thinking of going over to Nottingham by train to see the country of Robin Hood.

Blankney Hall, Digby, Lincolnshire circa 1920.

The Operations Room for the RCAF Digby Fighter Station was a couple of miles from the main Station. It was situated in Blankney Hall, an historic manor house which belonged to the Londesborough family estate. Lady Londesborough retained a small apartment at one end of the Hall. The Ops Room was set up in what had once been the Hall's enormous dining room, and the former livery stable had been converted into the Mess. RAF and

WAAF personnel and a few Canadian WDs were assigned living quarters above the Ops Room in the Hall.

The last half-dozen of us to arrive in Digby in late 1943 and early 1944 were billeted on the main Station pending the construction of some Nissen huts on the grounds of Blankney Hall. Our lodgings were in a small house originally designated as Married Quarters for Warrant Officers during peacetime. Upstairs there were a couple of bedrooms and the living-room on the ground floor slept three. Our heat was derived from one tiny fireplace which was abutted by a boiler in the kitchen. The theory was that if there was a fire burning in the fireplace, the heat generated would serve to heat up the water in the boiler. Given the restrictions imposed due to fuel rationing, our hot water supply was virtually non-existent. The truth is that we were seldom, if ever, warm, and most of us developed a first-hand acquaintance with chilblains – a painful condition we had only read about until our arrival in the north of England.

Feb. 7, 1944

After my arrival and welcome at Digby on Thursday/Friday of last week, I went to work with Helen and our shift on the Graveyard. It was the tail end of a two-week shift, which ended this morning at eight. We missed the bus to Lincoln, so hitch-hiked with some airmen on a military truck, caught the 9:10 a.m. train to Nottingham just by the hem of our garments and arrived in at 10:15. We were four Canadians, looking *very* lost. Two WAAF took us for coffee at The Granary, a little inn up a side lane. We got a room after that at the YWCA and then back to the Granery for lunch. Caught a bus out to the suburbs to see *Heaven Can Wait*. It's in technicolour and priceless. The laughter did us no harm.

And now back to the Y. for supper. Helen and I, having worked all night, feel like turning in early. The other two think differently and are definitely out "on the make". So we shall be parting company at seven o'clock – Helen and I to our chaste beds, the other two to what-have-you.

When we return to work tomorrow, we start a month of three 5 p.m. to midnight, three 8 a.m. to five p.m. shifts, alternately – then a fortnight of Graveyards. Once every six weeks we get a day off, and every three months our week of leave, with a "48" thrown in, if we don't take the latter during the three months.

In bright moonlight, Helen and I stole out with the coal scuttle to secure some fuel illegally from the pile behind the Canteen, and met others intent on the same task of petty pilfering. Shall not trouble to confess same to God on Sunday, since we are not penitent, and have every intention of repeating the performance again soon. One has to have a *little* heat in the evening – and our ration is not sufficient.

We took it in turn to go out two at a time during the blackout, after the truck had delivered its weekly ration of coal or coke to various points on the Station. We would then forage for chips wherever we found them and return to our quarters with the prospect of a little additional heat.

As luck would have it, the Station tennis courts were enclosed by a high wooden fence, not unlike wicker. To our delight we discovered that this material burned extremely well, and several expeditions were made under cover of darkness to hack off a piece here and another piece there and add it to our fuel supply. In due course we even grew bold enough to complete this operation in broad daylight.

It was only later that I learned by chance that the Station's Group Captain had been observing our fuel-gathering activity from the vantage point of his office window for weeks, yet had refrained from taking any disciplinary action. Small wonder that the men under Ernie McNab's command held him in such high regard. A veteran of the Battle of Britain, he was one of the first Canadians to shoot down an enemy aircraft. After two tours of Operations and a Distinguished Flying Cross, McNab was requested to take over command of Digby's RCAF Station. Undoubtedly his duties here must often have seemed tedious in contrast to past experiences; however he appeared to us to be a man of great equanimity and understanding.

Can now disclose that on the eve of our wedding we were in one of the heaviest of London's recent raids – very exciting! And the following Saturday, when we changed trains there, the situation was similar. Had often wondered how I would react. Not a bit as I had expected. You never feel that it's going to get **you** – which is the mercy of it, I suppose. Had had raids near and around before, but never **above**!

A man stopped us on the street today to ask what part of Canada we were from. Said he had come over with the 14th Black Watch in the last war and had been General Sir Frederick Loomis's batman.

Feb. 13th, 1944

At present, our only aim in life is to get back from work in order to start the fire in the grate in order to heat the water to wash clothes so we'll have something clean to wear in order to go to work! It's like the House that Jack built.

We came back from Nottingham on Tuesday in time for the five to midnight shift. Worked those hours for three evenings and slept until noon in the mornings. Friday, Saturday and today we worked from eight to five and coaxed the fire at night. That's the program for a month – three evenings and three days, alternately and then two weeks of Graveyard. Then a day off and we begin again. I hope to take one of my precious "48's" (We get four a year) and go down to London. That's on the 25th. The 32 hours off will be around March 7th, and Helen and I plan to go up to York for the day, on the chance of being able to meet some other WDs there, if they can get away. All ifs! It takes too long to get to London or I'd go there instead.

George McInnes, the lad who told George about the Tregenna Castle for our honeymoon, was killed the day before the wedding. He was to have come, and had just got himself engaged at Christmas to a girl in Montreal – by cable. Was sending her a ring by air mail. Then a gun backfired. I feel so sorry for his people -and the girl!

Snow today. Not enough to cover the ground but sufficient to make us wish for central heating. We got our annual ration of oranges today. We were to have had 4 (a pound) but since some went bad en route, we each get two. We're glad enough to see two, so there were no complaints! I ate one of mine right away and I'm keeping the other until I get really hungry for it. Wouldn't have believed that anything could taste so good.

The Salvation Army contributes a package of Sweet Caps a week, so with these and our weekly ration of forty at a reduced price, we are *just* going to manage for cigarettes. We have pooled the supplies from our parcels, so we have cocoa and soup and a snack at night. I had quite an amazing supply left from a parcel, so we have sandwiches, (bread courtesy of the Mess, but *they* don't know that!) and some soup, and a pudding.

Have had no mail except George's letters, for two weeks. I know there must be some on the way, but it's held up in London due to my change of location. I don't suppose anyone there knows what it's like not to get mail. I'd give a lot for one letter with a Canadian stamp on it. A fortnight isn't really a long time, but it seems so, when I know from what Mother said three weeks ago, that there must be letters and parcels on the way.

On the subject of dentistry – it seems so strange to go into a shack with a little stove in it and to sit on a folding chair to have one's teeth done. Certainly a contrast to being shot up to the eighth floor in an elevator and received in a room with thick rugs and magazines and mirrors *and* pink mouthwash... (I miss the mouthwash most – I used to love the taste!)

The work is proving interesting, though I have a lot to learn. Having come later than the others, I'm struggling on the lowest rung. When you know nothing, it's a temptation to bluff, but the English are quick to resent anything that approaches the blustering American type, so I have tried to keep my eyes and ears open and reserve comment.

They are also quick to approve of anyone who shows any signs of being "game", and I have been painfully aware that my every move is being weighed and considered. Have picked up a lot – even in one week – and everyone has been kind about showing me the ropes. At first it was hard to concentrate and even now I find that, in the midst of a most serious problem, a vision of Child's Restaurant on Windsor Street flashes through my mind or I start thinking about the snow on the hills at Piedmont; things that have nothing to do with the job at hand, and I have to pull my mind back from its wanderings.

Helen and I think there ought to be a new Bill of Emancipation for British women or a Bill of Rights to free them from their own ideas or something. Oh, they're doing a wonderful job, and all that, – don't mistake me – but their ideas are pre-historic. We had a discussion with the WAAF at lunch today and they were almost unanimous in the belief that there is no place for women at the top in either a trade or a profession. That we even ought to have male officers! They were outraged when I suggested mildly that they knew darned well that a woman officer was more likely to judge them on merit than on the length of skirt. Whew!

We have noticed, though, that the WAAF are not happy under their officers and we're sorry for them. We think *we* have the best leaders in the world and we don't mind who knows it! It's one of the things that was instilled in us at Rockcliffe, I guess; but no one would have persuaded us otherwise if it weren't the truth. We don't see anything wrong with the WAAF Officers – only with the ranks who aren't loyal to them. You can't have discipline in any organization if the people at the top don't command respect – and get it. So perhaps the fault *is* at the top. As for the rot about not having women as heads of industries and offices and so on – I am dogmatic! Perhaps the influence of Auntie Dot – who knows?

It took a certain amount of time for some of the WAAF at Blankney to realize that the Canadian WDs felt a little like strangers and also that many of us were homesick more often than we cared to admit. We also suspected that our sole WD Officer was not having an easy time of it, as the only Canadian woman in the Mess other than our Nursing Sister. For both of them we quickly developed great admiration and affection.

Although in due course we made some fast friends among the WAAF at Digby, initially it was not a bed of roses. For one thing, there was a marked difference between WAAF Officers and their Other Ranks. We Canadians, on the other hand, respected the King's Commission while on duty, but were more casual at other times. Our WD Officer, when she came to inspect our quarters, made sure that we had cleaned and tidied. She had no more interest in compulsive polishing that we had, and after Inspection would remove her cap, sit on a bed, have a cup of coffee, smoke a cigarette and chat with us informally. This casual attitude (and our acceptance of it) was perceived as Very Bad Form by the WAAFs.

In all fairness, there were mitigating circumstances involved. For one thing we were fresh new arrivals from Canada, whereas our WAAF counterparts of whatever rank had lived through the Battle of Britain and its aftermath. Also we were receiving letters and parcels from home, and the Canadian boys on the Station gave us a warm and enthusiastic welcome

from the moment we arrived. As well, being free of any domestic
responsibilities, it was possible for us to strike out for other parts of the U.K.
almost like holidaying tourists, to visit relatives or friends or to link up with
other Canadians. Into the bargain, our pay was slightly higher than the
WAAFs' and this, too, added to the general sense of negativity that came our
way from some quarters.

Feb. 16, 1944

Helen is away on a "48", so I am hunting alone, so to speak. One of the Corporals and I went over to see our WD Officer today. She has been laid up for a week in her quarters with a "Strept" throat. Poor little dear was wrapped in a blanket, sitting over a fire in the grate. She's the only WD Officer on the Station, so I think she was glad to have some Canadians come in. She's from Outremont – S/O Grace Findlay.

I whispered to Jamie (Jean Jamieson) before we went in that I supposed we ought to salute, and Jamie said, "Of course." The gloves I am wearing are the gift of the Salvation Army, and were meant for a man. So I look rather like Mickey Mouse when I salute. And Miss Findlay laughed, which was the desired result, though we hadn't intended to cheer her up quite so soon after entering. She has done a lot for us since she came back from her Leave and she's the sort that doesn't *ask* how come we have a fire nearly every day. As Jamie says, "We have to live, don't we?"

Have a new account of the way the Army mind works. Was sent for to attend a Dental Parade, which I did – to be told that my records said I had three wisdom teeth to be extracted. Remembering something about a double dose of injections, 'way back when, I said nothing and obediently went in to the dentist's office.

When he discovered that the only wisdom tooth left isn't even through, he was irate. I was not perturbed, having nothing (shall I say?) to *lose*, and said that if the Army said I had to have three wisdom teeth out, why there wasn't much I could do about it, was there, and when did he propose to start? My records were immediately written up to date. Such speed I have never seen. And then it turned out, when the dentist tried to fill a tooth that hasn't been in my head for ten years, that I had someone else's X-rays, as well as my own, among my papers. He found that the cavity shown in the X-ray was Joe Someone-or-other's! Ah, me – at what price efficiency! Am waiting now to hear that they want my tonsils, which were also removed ten years ago.

Have added a scarf to my sleeping suit of heavy socks, sweater and bathrobe. Would wear my slippers as well, but they are what keep my ears warm, so I can't spare them for my feet.

Tonight we are trying to bully the fire into burning. Newspaper is scarce, kindling almost non-existent and the coal and coke damp. We alternately invoke the gods and curse. But the gods are deaf and the fire won't burn. We had the usual inspection of our billets today and they think we might spend more time on the brass door-knobs. So I have polished everything in sight tonight. We go to work at 7:40 a.m. on the Transport, which means six o'clock rising and believe me, this *is* England's Darkest Hour – and mine as well.

We came from work at midnight last night, had our corn flakes, sausages, potatoes and beans in the Mess at one and got to bed, as is usual on this shift, at two. Today we began the three-day watch of eight to five, so this fifty-six hour week calls for fortitude.

A few of us were allowed off to go to the dance for an hour last night and I went, reluctantly. Of all things, met the boys from the place where I was before I came over here. They are lonely and homesick. Three of them just got married at Christmas and I was the first acquaintance they had met on this Station; so I heard all their woes and agreed that out of my limited experience I thought marriage a wonderful institution. We also talked about our former Station. Some of them I had known well – others only by voice over the 'phone. Was certainly glad I'd dropped in at the dance.

The air-crew are usually a good sort. I don't think there's anything much more pathetic than a lonesome pilot. Some of our lads who have been here awhile have just received bars to their DFC – so there is much rejoicing.

Helen got some pink material for curtains and the room is beginning to look lived-in. We have a cupboard and several little crates and cases, which we have covered with the same material and which brought us a good mark. Family photos deck the tables. We bought some prints in Lincoln, so the walls, which were clean but bare, are now more cheerful. We are not too overcrowded, we three. Thank heaven they don't know about two-decker beds over here and we aren't telling them. Our beds here are cots – with mattresses (called biscuits) which come in three pieces, of course!

We had not been at Digby very long before the WAAF Officer-of-the-Day arrived to inspect our billets and, seeing nothing out of order, ran her hand across the top of a door. As a result we were Confined to Barracks for seven days and were expected to wax our already well-polished floors every evening after supper; but though we obediently remained in our quarters, we made sure that only one of us did the waxing on each successive night, so that our individual misery was of relatively short duration. And if the WAAF Officer's intention was to try to improve our attitude, this particular application of "Jankers" – the term we used for disciplinary measures of this sort – only served to unite us in our sense of outrage at such

*a pointless attempt to maintain esprit de corps in the ranks, and to establish
a position of authority.*

Feb. 22, 1944

Every day is Ash Wednesday here. So tomorrow, the first day of Lent, will be little different from any other day. We have all the materials suitable for acts of contrition, and most of our waking hours are spent on our knees in front of the two-by-four fireplace. We have a little electric toaster now, which will heat a small kettle of water and I have at last completed the washing left over from my Leave – a pint of hot water at a time. We found the chimney flue last night, too, and cleared it out. We didn't exactly look like Water Babies when we were finished, but what price glory?

We have a pet now – a little brown mouse. He kept us awake the other night, chewing up a paper bag and scattering pellets all over the floor. Didn't mind that, nor even the noise; but the next morning I found he had eaten half my week's chocolate ration – which is going a bit too far, I'd say. I don't think we'll do anything about Jimmy, but that's the last food he gets.

When we came back from Nottingham two weeks ago, Helen found a very squashed mouse (very dead, too) in her knapsack. We'd had to sit on our luggage, failing to find a seat on the train, so I suppose that's how the little fellow died.

Monday we went over to the Airmen's Mess to a dance and met our Canadian friends again. The party was a bit flat though; three of the boys didn't come back Sunday night.

Poor old London has been getting it again. The only comfort to anyone is that Berlin is taking such a beating. What misery there must be in that city!

Sunday evening I had an hour off from work and I walked up to the cross-roads at the next village. It was the first time I'd seen the village and I was very impressed with the quaintness of it. Four rows of grey stone cottages and a sign-post in the middle, a little stone school-house, complete with thatched roof and ding-dong bell and a tiny church at the gate to the Estate to which all this belongs. Lovely evening. Blue sky, setting sun and everything so green in that last light. Very peaceful and unhurried.

Time for me to get my mug and line up for a drink. We pay sixpence a week toward a canteen and during "break" at ten and three o'clock, we may have tea, coffee, Bovril or Ovaltine. I have my name on my mug, but today someone walked off with my "irons" (knife, fork and spoon) so I must be on the lookout for some.

Left here at eight Saturday morning, caught the nine o'clock train from Lincoln, changed at Grantham. A very kind RAF Squadron Leader found me a seat and when we got to London at 2:00, he piloted me across town in the Tube, involving three changes, and bought me tea and a bun while we waited for the southern train. I would still be riding on the inner circle of the tube, going round and round, were it not for him. (Permanent Forces, spent years in India, very British.)

Caught the 2:30 train to the south coast. One of my travelling companions was Mrs. Halford – the Second-in-Command of the Canadian Officers' Club in the Haymarket. She was also going down for the Regiment's dance. Very kindly gave me her card and asked me to stay with her in London if I'm ever there by myself "Only, don't come this week – I've no roof on my flat". The ravages of war. She was obviously glad to get out of town, if only for a day or two, for a rest from it all. Her husband is C.O. of one of the Stations near where I am.

George and I stayed at a hotel near the Battalion. Went to the dance early, to be there when the Brigadier and Colonel arrived, but they were very late, so the music started without them. It made for a very long evening for us. The dance was held in the Royal Pavilion – a tremendous monument built by George IV when he was Prince Regent. It's huge, very ornate and *very* ugly. Great red and green drapes, horrible Chinese murals, chandeliers, and gilt paint on everything.

Sunday we had dinner at a nearby hotel and I began to recover from the starvation of the day before. Travelling and eating cannot be done at the same time. That afternoon we did something unique. We went to see a movie- our first together – and saw Fred Astaire in *The Sky's the Limit.*

George had to be on parade at 8:00 a.m., so I caught an early train and was in London by ten. Got a bus to Trafalgar Square and walked along to Pall Mall on an errand for George – to buy a Commando knife. But the shop isn't there this week and all I could do was stand and watch the sweeping and digging and moving and carting. It was like a very sad beaver colony. There was an Irish Setter whose master had been killed in the raid, and the dog was sitting beside a heap of bricks and plaster, shaking like a leaf. The Bobbie said that if I talked to the dog for a minute, he'd stop shivering. So I talked to him, and he did settle down and licked my hand. Poor fellow!

I turned back to Trafalgar Square, walked in a circle for a bit and then went to the Canadian Girls' Club for some coffee. I took a bus along the Strand and got off before I reached the Daily Express, so that I could have the pleasure of walking down Fleet Street.

From there I walked back to Kingsway and through the Temple Bar court-yard to Lincoln's Inn Fields. In front of the Bar a Bobbie stopped all the traffic to let a judge through and saluted him. The judge was clad in black robes and wing collar, etc. and he looked like a bit of the 18th Century in the midst of blitzed London. I expected to see Charles Lamb or old Sam Johnson appear at any minute. I wonder what Lamb would have written about, in this day and age.

The buildings in and about Temple Bar are so very solid-looking that one has the feeling that war or no war, they'll be there for another thousand or so years; and that the events of the moment are not really of any great importance. A sort of "men may come and men may go...." feeling, and then, when one realizes that every night thousands of people take their blankets down to the Underground 'way below the earth to sleep there, the events of the moment seem very important.

At Air Ministry I had tea in the Canteen with a couple of WDs whom I hadn't seen since the wedding. Went by tube to King's Cross to get the four o'clock train. After a number of changes, I finally got to Lincoln just in time to see the 8:15 bus pull out. It had snowed over the week-end and of course I had no rubbers – not that they would have helped much.

Mary and George Buch on Leave, early 1944.

There I was in a strange place. No torch. No rubbers. No bus!

I stood out in front of the bus terminal for awhile, wondering how to kill two hours. Began to feel like a permanent fixture – monumental – with frozen feet – statue of the Irate Traveller, presented by victims of the Great Northern Railway. Finally wandered into the lounge of a nearby hotel and felt like barking at the people who stared at me, when I was really dying to talk to somebody. Ordered a couple of gins, since there wasn't any beer, and got more and more irritated at the circumstances which had driven me to drink alone! When I finally did get to the bus, Helen was there. She had been to a movie, so we waited the last three quarters of an hour together.

March 2, 1944

Tomorrow I leave at noon for London for a fling with George. We'll be staying at either the Dorchester or the Strand Palace and for 48 hours time will stand still, and our lives will once more be concentric. No cold. No war. No eating from a mess-tin or drinking from a tin mug. Instead there'll be music and a hot bath and breakfast in bed. Dancing and civvies and a tablecloth. No loneliness, and all the things one pretends one doesn't miss, before it's back to billets, to orders, inspections, parades and – for George – battle. All very dramatic in the movies, but in real life it's pure unadulterated Hell. I wonder whether, when we get home, we'll forget all this – or ever take peace for granted.

March 6th, 1944

Friday morning dawned beautifully... (I saw it). Pay Parade and a minute 'Spection to see which cupboard the dust was brushed into and then a quick lunch. After that a queue for the bus at noon and another queue for the train. Stood all the way to London for my rendez-vous with George.

We saw the Changing of the Guard at Buckingham Palace. (Christopher Robin went down with Alice!). It's probably the best parade of polished leather and brass and the most precise drill to be seen. A good show. Walked back along The Mall to Trafalgar Square and up to Piccadilly Circus. Had lunch at the Piccadilly Hotel and wandered about during the early afternoon, followed by tea at the hotel and then started off for the show. Saw *Love for Love* – Congreve's piece with John Gielguid. Very good entertainment. Costumes lovely and all well done.

The theatres are out by 9:00 as a rule, so we just managed to get back to the hotel for a late dinner. London was as I first saw it – lit up by moonlight – exquisite!

Sunday afternoon we set out to see Westminster Abbey. Indescribable! The Tomb of the Unknown Soldier was perhaps the most moving sight among the memorials to England's known and famous dead. Big Ben struck three as we came out. A friendly clock, Old Ben. I felt as though I'd known him for years! [*due to the familiar time-signal on the BBC Overseas News broadcasts to Canada.*]

We crossed St. James' Park to the Canadian Girls' Club, where there is a tea for Canadians on Sunday afternoons. Left there to go to King's Cross for my five o'clock train. Jerry kept his distance, so our tin hats were not needed – fortunately.

The sequel, though, is part of Fate's sense of humour. The trains were all late – as usual – and I got to Lincoln too late for the last bus at 10:15, so I had to spend the night in the station. The Railway Transport Officer gave me a chit to get a bunk in the YWCA's canteen. English Stations make Bonaventure look like luxury itself, so you can imagine that I was not sorry to get the seven a.m.

bus to work, where I could wash and eat, not having had a bite since tea the previous day. Have yet to find out whether I get "Jankers" for being late.

———————

Indeed a red-letter day! Bags of Canadian mail from all across the Dominion. Heard from several of RCAF girls, three from the Queen's crowd and so on. All very good!

Today I'm all of twenty-two, but since we're on the Graveyard this fortnight it might as well be my *ninetieth* and I'd feel no difference.

Our WD Officer took Helen and me by the hand today and led us to Stores for an issue of WAAF underclothing. They asked us about sizes and, since Helen and I are like Mr. and Mrs. Jack Spratt, it was rather disconcerting to find that there was only *one size* of anything on hand. I thought S/O Findlay would collapse with laughter. Helen's pyjamas are too small and mine are like tents on me, but, of course, too short. We were also issued smocks and Helen has to let hers out, while mine fits, but is too long. And so it goes...

It turns out that Miss Findlay graduated from the Montreal School for Teachers in 1925 and went on to become an authority in teaching circles on the instruction of retarded children. I thought there was something familiar about her name and face and now realize why.

———————

We've been able to get some snatches of sleep at night at work, so the change is almost as good as a whole night's sleep. And better than eight hours of intensive concentration. I don't believe anyone of us will live to see the kind of world we hope for. It will take years to repair, but perhaps some of the pieces of our dreams will be salvaged, as long as the world moves forward after the war...

Spring has come! Helen and I took a long promenade this morning, instead of going to bed as we should. We walked about four miles to the nearest little village – two rows of cottages on the border of a huge estate. I fed a lump of sugar to a pony who will now love me forever. The primroses and the snowdrops are out and we saw the first crocuses. We climbed over tomb-stones in the little village church-yard and picked some wild flowers to bring back with us.

Blue, blue sky and white clouds racing. A very strong wind, which blew all the cobwebs away. (Night shifts *do* leave cobwebs!) We watched the silly ducks in the farm yards and talked to all the horses we saw grazing. The estate is beautiful. A little lake lies near the Big House, with swans – would you believe it – out in the flat country of this 'shire. We came back ready to sleep and quite refreshed, as well.

Have just come in this evening from supplementing our coal ration. Took a bucket and picked up bits and pieces which had fallen near the fences when the coal cart came by. A heavenly night, tonight. One always wonders what activity the darkness will bring.

And now, at eleven to the Mess for some corn flakes and sausage. If I never saw another sausage or a piece of pork-and-bean pie, it would be far, far too soon! Then on the transport to work. I like that ride, through the night along English lanes. Then the spell of it is broken when the truck lurches to a stop and we all tumble out ... to work.

One more thing worthy of note. We had a fried egg for breakfast. A completely lovely day!

There is an indescribable tension and intensity of action – even the newspapers are full of it. The Irish question is creating a peculiar sort of bedlam. The feelings are mixed. It seemed inevitable that Ireland should be closed off, but then the new step is an infringement of neutrality which is, in turn, an infringement of democracy. If I were a native of Eire, I'm sure I'd feel bitter. After all, Britain would have had a thin time without Eire's exports and if the Germans had the advantage of position for their Fifth Column, the British had the advantage of trade, which makes it a deadlock. However, the statement that he who is not with us is against us was never truer than it is today. And I suppose in a world such as this there can be no neutrals; but what a sorry mess! I wonder if we will ever learn ?

Yesterday Helen and I cycled up to the Pay Office in the next village – about five miles away. The wind was against us coming back, and since it's the first real exercise I've had for weeks, I was exhausted. But the fresh air did us good and when we finally got to bed at noon, we slept until eleven p.m.! Our resolution is to do this more often. We get tired enough at work, but it's a fatigue of the nerves more than anything else – and our nerves are very much like nutmeg-graters now. We won't be sorry to get back on the day-shift, – for all that the nights are more interesting and exciting.

Two of the girls broke down this week. But that won't happen to us. I'm actually putting on weight, though perhaps one wouldn't notice. Our meals consist of an endless number of breakfasts, since we are asleep during the other meals – lunch and tea. So life is one large piece of toast – plus porridge – and it does make for increased pounds and ounces.

We are qualifying for the Spam-eater's ribbon, otherwise known here as the EBGO (Every Bastard's Got One.) It's for eighteen months' service, and the Clasp – a Maple Leaf – represents sixty days service outside Canada. (The eighteen months is for beans twice a day and the sixty days counts for Spam.) The ribbon itself is the subject of much ridicule in these quarters, and the RAF looks upon it in much the same light as the Yanks' ribbons.

In England, where most people have been in the Line of Fire more times than they care to talk about, and where three years service means you're just a

"Sprog" (rookie), a ribbon such as the one most Canadians must now sport is almost impertinent. It might have been a bit more tactful to at least wait until after the War.

March 12, 1944

Of all the things anyone could possibly need, it's *letters* that do the most good. Things go wrong, one's temper gets shorter and shorter. We become intolerant of the food, the weather, the place, the people. It is, in fact, a Blue World. And then, when we have just about disproved the theory of the will to survive, and tried the patience of everyone around us, *mail* arrives. No one remarks on the sudden change of attitude and outlook. We all know. Word has come from halfway across the world and, figuratively, the sun is shining again.

Off to breakfast now. Ten to one it's sausage and mash!

PART SIX

Settling In
March – May 1944

On our highly prized 36-hour passes, we often headed to York for a pre-arranged rendez-vous with other WD's stationed at #62 Base. Trains were unreliable and time was limited so we hitch-hiked both ways. Almost the only vehicles on the road belonged to the Army, and getting a ride never seemed to pose much of a problem for us. Needless to say, we never ventured forth on our own. Even travelling in pairs there was probably an element of risk involved, but it certainly never struck us as anything more than minimal, since we were all in uniform.

March 22, 1944

Helen and I had a splendid 32 hour Leave. Came back in high spirits, which only goes to prove that there is something to be gained by giving people time

Mary and Nancy Tauton – RCAF, W.D. cousins of Mary Buch.

off to get away from the Station for awhile. Not that anyone doubted it.

We finished work at 8:00 a.m. Monday. Caught the eight o'clock bus to Lincoln by missing breakfast, then the 9:15 train to Doncaster to change for York. We were due in York at 12:30. At twelve I happened to ask someone what station we were going through. When he said "Grantham", my comment was that there is a place called Grantham in Lincolnshire, too. To make a long story short, we had been admiring Yorkshire – or so we thought- but meantime were travelling *South*. Another hour and we would have been in London!

We had lunch in Peterborough. Shall not forget the irony of looking up to see a poster which said "YORK.... It's quicker by rail". Some of the other girls were hitch-hiking to their destinations.

The train to York from Peterborough was in on time, so we were there by five o'clock – exhausted. Mona and Cherry had arrived from Knaresborough just before, and Mary Taunton had said she'd try to get in by six. We were in the bar when she came at seven. Started our dinner then and, in the middle of it, who should arrive but Nancy Taunton, Mary's sister. She's at Mona's Station – a Code and Cypher Officer who hasn't been over very long. Seems rather a dear. She whipped away to meet someone, and we spent the rest of the evening talking like magpies.

Mary's train to Leeming left at 11:00 and I went over to the railway station with her. It certainly was good to see her. She is apparently very busy, and very happy. She's crazy about the work and, altogether, life is good. What a marvelous type Mary is! She hitch-hiked in to York, by the way. I guess it's only dumb people like us that think it's quicker by rail!

Mona and I talked half the night. Breakfast-time came far too soon. Our train left at ten, so arrived back at Erewhon by four – in time for tea, and work at five. Thank heaven we're through the Graveyard Shift for another month! We can eat again now – something besides corn flakes and toast.

I guess there'll be no more trips to Brighton – the whole coast is a restricted area, from the Wash to St. Ives'.

Had our baptism of fire recently. Very thrilling! No damage (except to "Jerry"). Jean Houston was in the bathtub and the rest of us were getting ready to go to work or packing up to go away, when the lights went out. From then on we began to enjoy ourselves. The element of suspense and all that.

Now that our Nissen huts are almost ready for us, we are beginning to think about moving. Perhaps next month. We'll be out near work then and there will be no transport journey involved. Can't say that we are anxious to leave our quarters, but it will be a different life and variety is not to be sneezed at. We were just beginning to get the linoleum into a decent condition, with wax and elbow-grease.

March 25, 1944

Most of my letters are written at odd moments on shift when things are quiet(er), or just before I turn in... or on the Graveyard, when everything is upside down. But it's seven o'clock on a beautiful spring evening. The windows are wide open, the tulips in bloom. (Yes, and primroses are there!)

March 26th, 1944

Beautiful Sunday morning – not unlike a day in May on the Macdonald Campus. The lawns are perhaps a little rougher and the elms are very big and very old. There's a nest of baby rabbits under a bush near the window of the "drawing-room-that-was" in the Big House. The Shetland pony has been allowed out of his paddock and he's grazing on the grounds, up and down between the house and the lodge.

There are dogs of all shapes and sizes in the stables, and not a few who live at the Manor. M'Lady takes her favorite two or three out for a walk Sunday morning, so she ought soon to be going by. One of the dogs is a Whippet or something. Two of the big fellows are Great Danes – the kind C. Aubrey Smith had in *Little Lord Fauntleroy*. He called them "Get Off the Rug" and "You, Too", and when he spoke, they'd slowly get up and lumber off. And then there's a little bag of wool that they say is a dog – I can never tell whether "Pixie" is coming or going. Don't know how she knows – herself!

March 30th, 1944

Busy as the day – or the night – is long. Have been putting in some overtime, and sleeping odd hours to make up. Reading everything I can lay hands on in my spare time. I'd give anything for a whiff of Spring at home. The exile grows nostalgic, even after a mere four months!

Inspection of our billets today brought an "Excellent" today, which we find too sissy. We didn't want to break our record of "Very Good". So no more floor-polishing for a while.

Leading Airwoman Helen Woodcroft and Mary Buch (left) cycling in the countryside near RCAF Station, Digby, Lincolnshire, 1944.
Collection of M. Jean Houston

The mad month of March is doing its best to go out like a lion; but it's a feeble attempt. We shed our greatcoats this week and I feel much as a serpent must when he sheds his skin.

I had my Medical Board for my Commission yesterday. S/O Findlay saw the Wing Officer in London two weeks ago and there was no hope of any vacancy – to say nothing of the hordes in front of me waiting in line.

The Groupie (Group Captain, in proper English) was to inspect the new huts today. They aren't quite ready for occupation yet, but the floors must be waxed if "He" is to come, so you know how our spare time was spent today.

Helen and I are going to cycle out to watch the boys land, and I'll post this on the way.

Last night Helen and I went for a cycle out along country lanes. Just at take-off time, it's heavenly. The boys are usually waiting beside their kites and their greetings are cheerfully casual. We usually dismount at the runway and watch them take off, as they gain first speed and then height, across the field and over the farm-houses, until finally they are just dark shapes going down the golden highway of the setting sun into the horizon. Nothing but the fading drone to break the stillness of the spring evening.

The return is an even more satisfying operation than the take-off. The red and green port and starboard lights, the myriads of wings, like electric eyes in the dark. And what a relief when they are all safely home again!

This evening we walked out to the Sick Quarters. Our Officer (Grace Findlay) is ill again with a "cold in the doze". Popped in to see her for five minutes. A beautiful walk back – cold and windy, but most refreshing.

Tomorrow I hope to hitch-hike to town with one of the WAAF Corporals to go to the morning service at Lincoln Cathedral. There are no buses Sunday morning, so I hope we get a lift. Lincoln is a most surprising place. A hill rises suddenly from the plains of the 'shire. The town is built on the side of the hill and the Cathedral is at the top, visible from miles away. (Reminds me a bit of

A Lancaster Bomber over the city of Lincoln. From painting by David Cuppleditch

Quebec and the Bastion.) My vivid imagination dreams up a picture of a pilgrimage wending its way up the hill to the Cathedral – perhaps in the time of Richard II. Not a likely picture, perhaps, but pleasing to my mind's eye!

> *Early in April 1944, armies were being moved towards the launching sites, the Continent was being "softened up" by our bombers, and every effort had been made to ensure that all ranks were in their places. Nevertheless, if a couple were both due for Leave, this was arranged through their respective Commanding Officers*

April 7th, 1944
Good Friday

We heard yesterday that all Leave has been cancelled by the Air Ministry. Also all "48's", and we are restricted to an area twelve miles from camp.

April 8th, 1944

The wild daffies are out in great profusion. Beautiful. The blaze of gold in the fields and gardens and beside the hedges is something to behold. And there's a nest of rabbits in our hedge – baby ones – for Easter. Cute as they can be!

April 20, 1944

The week before was one long headache. Phoning George – sometimes twice a day. Wiring, getting a letter from his Adjutant to my Adjutant, and Miss Findlay pulling all sorts of wires for a Compassionate Leave. My Leave form required nothing less than the Air Marshal's signature.

The outcome of it was that last Saturday I left for a week's Leave near George's unit. His room-mate, Don Menzies, met me at the station at nine that night and took me out to wine, dine and dance. Also to explain that George would be late returning from his course.

I got back to the hotel around 11:00, unpacked, had a hot bath and tried to sleep. At 2:00 a.m. in walked the *muddiest* man I 've ever seen, with the news that there would be no use in my staying after Wednesday. So the next day we wired Camp to say I'd be returning for duty four days early.

George was on duty a good bit of the three days that followed, but he was allowed to stay at the hotel at night, and we did have dinner together, although twice he went back to the job in the evening. On Wednesday morning George put me on the 8:00 train and I got back to camp in time to get ready for the Graveyard shift. The Station was a little perturbed at an Airwoman returning early from her Leave – but obviously I had no choice! I had secured time only because George was to have it.

April 21, 1944

Today I had a Kit Inspection, having been away in January when the others had theirs. Had to lay out everything on my bed – washed, ironed, shined, polished, and so forth. Jamie (Jean Jamieson) asked S/O Findlay to come a bit early and have a cup of tea, which she did. You have gathered by now that we don't like to work too hard on our house! But today we really went to town on it. For once it looked very cosy. No butts or stray magazines lying around and everything polished, even the taps – which is a concession! Also a roaring fire and "a kettle on the hob".

Jamie and I went out and gathered flowers – violets, daffies, black-thorn, wild almond blossoms – and then I got rash and tried an experiment. Dad had sent me some "Tea Bisk" in a parcel, so I went over to the NAAFI [*Navy, Army, Air Force Institute*] canteen and asked if I might use their oven. They allowed me fifteen minutes, so I whipped back for the Klim [*powdered milk*] and set to. Result: Some very good baking-powder biscuits! Anything with white flour in it would be good, after the brown hay we use here.

We also had some real butter, thanks to my ration card and some honey. It was like Old Home Week. Helen had some tea and we have plates now and of course our mugs – and sugar from the Mess, and Klim. It was super fun and with the afternoon sun pouring in to what we call our living-room – and the flowers, and the glorious day – it was very pleasant.

Incidentally, my Kit is "all present and accounted for", thank goodness! Things have a habit of disappearing and I haven't had a proper check since I came over. It's a relief to know that I'm not going to be charged with "loss or destruction of Air Force Property".

The Saracen's Head Pub

What do you think of an officer who invites her Other Ranks out to lunch and buys them Scotch and beer with their meal? Miss Findlay and our Canadian Nursing Sister Kaines, from Winnipeg, took us to the Saracen's Head in Lincoln last week and we had a thoroughly enjoyable time.

Every six weeks we were given thirty-six hours off – from 8:00 a.m. till the following afternoon at five. Apart from this, it was forty-two days straight through without a break. I suspect we might have done this more cheerfully had we thought it necessary to work such long hours – hours which often seemed almost endless when the weather closed in. The theory appears to have been that an excess of leisure time for Other Ranks might lead to an outbreak of "trouble" – a euphemism for getting pregnant – and was therefore something to be avoided at all costs.

There were more than enough of us WDs and WAAFs so that when things were"quiet" we could all have had more time off than we actually got. As things were, we worked an average of fifty-six hours a week for six weeks; although some weeks we were on the job for as much as seventy hours. This is not taking into account such routine matters as Kitting Parades, Dental Parades or a variety of extra Inspections. These Parades were held during the day, and attendance was compulsory, regardless of whether or not we had been on the midnight shift and needed our sleep.

Our WD Officer, perceiving that our morale was in tatters, encouraged us by arranging activities, such as baseball, which would take us to nearby Stations. She and the Nursing Sister also invited anyone not on duty to meet them for lunch in Lincoln – a six mile bus ride from the Station – or to cycle to a nearby pub for a Ploughman's Lunch. On our first outing we were understandably a little reticent, but when S/O Findlay called the waiter over and said, " A round of drinks, please... and the bill to me," we got the message that we really were " Off Duty " and, if we were not exactly on equal footing, it was made clear that we could let our hair down and relax.

April 24th, 1944

It's not solitude so much as privacy that one craves, and a straight forty-eight hours or more in a place of seclusion would not make up for the lack of time to oneself over a period of months.

One of the factors over which we had no control was the communal nature of life in uniform. We worked, lived and ate with the same people – day in and day out – all of us together. There was no real "going home" at the end of a shift, leaving the job behind us. We could – and did – go off on bicycles in two's or three's if weather permitted. The alternative was Group Living – radios playing, someone ironing, the rest of us chatting back and forth.

We had no trouble coping with a major crisis; however, as is so often the case, in such close quarters, it was the small things that sometimes got us down. Who had borrowed whose curlers without permission? Whose turn was it to forage for fuel ? In the extreme, these inconsequential trivialities could lead to a full-blown confrontation or to silent sulking. In a life where, as we often remarked, " Everything not forbidden is compulsory". How could anyone manage to find an hour's quiet contemplation?

Often when we'd be out biking, there would be prolonged periods of silence, and I suspect most of us were availing ourselves of the chance to indulge in our own personal daydreams or simply to let our minds go completely blank. Either way, it was as close as we were able to come to any kind of privacy and these moments, away from the crowd, were something most of us valued immeasurably.

April 26, 1944

How beautiful the countryside is in April! There are flowers by the acre, gardens all a blaze of glory. The sky so blue, the trees just coming out, the hedges and fields are intensely green. Hot sun and cool winds – it's wonderful.

Four of us left the Station at one o'clock for Lincoln, then onto another bus that took us to the city limits. From there we hitch-hiked. Got two rides very easily. One in a van delivering Modess at every cross-roads and one in a jeep with a Captain in the Royal Engineers, who wasn't delivering anything and drove us right to the Market Square of Nottingham, where the YWCA is.

Nottingham seems very much friendlier than Lincoln. We weren't even allowed to pay our fare on the buses there, because we're in the Service – a rule the conductresses made up for themselves, unofficially! Everyone was very kind about giving us directions. As for hitch-hiking – it's *the* way to travel. Military cars will nearly always give us a lift – and vans if they have room. The men in the car this morning said that hitch-hiking in England was "not done" before 1939. All the Service people seem to, now. I don't think girls would in Canada, much, except perhaps outside a city. I can picture being stranded a hundred miles from nowhere, at home. Here the distances are short.

While in Nottingham I had planned to visit the aging uncle of a Winnipeg friend of Marion Strang's, but arrived at the address I'd been given only to learn from the lady who opened the door that he had died the week before. Under the circumstances, I might have felt more awkward than I did, had it not been for the very warm welcome given me by Mrs. Durham and her husband – perhaps the warmest I'd had since coming to England.

She had a book of autographs of Service people who had visited the house during World War I, and it turned out that a friend and classmate of my father's, Stuart Forbes, had signed his name in the book with a list of wounds and decorations after it. So I also had the privilege of inscribing my name and rank (no wounds or decorations) in the book, before heading back to meet my friends for dinner.

I joined the others at 6:45 and we went to the Flying Horse for dinner. Having worked all the previous night without a break, we were weary, so we turned in early and I slept like a log. We were up by 9:30, had coffee in the same quaint shop as last time, and then Jamie and I took a bus to the outskirts of Nottingham as we had a meeting at six. Got a ride in no time and were back in Lincoln by lunchtime.

Saw lots of Gypsies today. I'd seen them before, but never so many. Their caravans are sometimes parked at the road-side while they cook a meal over a fire, just as I had read about. Their skins are very dark and we are told that they actually are descendants of the Romany tribes of Gypsies that used to wander across Europe. They are eligible for War Service now – when they can be caught. They seem to earn their living travelling from one fair to another, helping with the side-shows. And in the Fall they do the harvesting for local farmers. I can think of ways I'd rather live. The ones we saw had a whole string of ponies and horses tied behind their caravans.

April 26th – (Later)

The Air Ministry says our Station needs to buck up in the line of Progressive Training for WAAF – a sort of "extra-curricular activities" scheme. All the WAAF authorities can guess from this is that their chicks are not putting their "spare" time to good use. Air Ministry's idea is to provide training for a post-war world. The WAAF are satisfied if they can keep us out of mischief.

Jamie and I went to a meeting tonight to represent the WDs. It consisted largely of proposals to teach the girls Mothercraft and gardening. I'm sorry! At the moment I'm interested in neither. It was made clear that the girls are not to be instructed in anything which might help them to get a job in a "Man's World" after the war. (One must assume that the woman's place is always in the home. The fact that -unless we introduce polygamy – there aren't going to be enough men to have all our women safely tucked away, each in her own kitchen, seems to have no bearing on it. Or that there will be at least five women for every man, after the war is finished and over).

We are still shackled with the (I think) outdated idea that women must be limited in their instruction, lest the competition be too keen.

May 4th, 1944

What a time *this* has been! Two weeks of Graveyard with something under sixty hours' sleep – all told. And last Thursday the wind blew in a "Distinguished Visitor" – Wing Officer K. Walker. We heard about her advent in the morning when we came off duty, so the day was spent – not sleeping – but cleaning up the billets. S/O Findlay brought her around at six p.m. and she sat on one of the bunks and chatted with us for about half an hour. She was unbearably cheerful. (She *would* come on the hottest day yet!) And she told us how lucky we were, to be where we are. Described the life of the London WDs. Meanwhile we'd give our eye-teeth to be there.

S/O Findlay gave us a super opportunity to open our own private Second Front and we jumped in with both feet; only to be firmly, if politely, given the brush-off. So from the Wing Officer's point of view it was just another Inspection and from ours it was a wash-out. We were all primed and briefed for the occasion – with no result. I'd have given the Staff Officer more credit for a bit of interest, but we've "had it"! A shattering blow to morale; however, we've been far too busy to think about it.

At the hotel in York, Mona and I ordered a Scotch at the bar, only to find that someone had paid for it. Turned out to be the little man over in the corner, who told us he had been born in Canada and was delighted to see some Canadian girls, etc., etc. We went into the dining room – Mona and I – and in a few minutes the little man came in and talked to us again. He told us he's a jockey and he's been riding for forty-seven years. Won a high stake last week and was off to buy as many more horses as he could find. He has a place in Berkshire and said his wife would give us all the milk we could drink – pails and pails of it – if we ever dropped in. You gather that Mona and I hardly got a word in edgewise. After our little man had left us and we went to pay our bill, we found that he had not only looked after that, but had paid for another double Scotch!

The head waiter said "You know who that was, don't you?" We confessed our ignorance and he told us it was "Brusher" Herbert – apparently internationally known as a rider. He certainly had told us a lot about racing. He claims the game is far fairer here than in either America or Australia. Says the idea here is for the best horse to win and that racing elsewhere is a tricky business. We were a bit startled at his friendliness, but it just goes to show that one meets all kinds! A nice little man ...

Helen wondered why her friend Ted hadn't telephoned her when she was on her "32". When we got back to camp there was word that he is Missing. The night of the 27th of April. He's a Squadron-Leader – Ted Blenkinsop from Victoria. His mother is an S/O in the WDs and Ted just got the D.F.C. last week. Had almost finished his second tour of Ops with the Pathfinder Force. We're hoping to hear that he's been washed up on some shore. There's a good chance. It's a rough break for Helen, because she was to meet him next week.

PART SEVEN

Notes from a Nissen Hut
May – August 1944

May 4th, 1944
(continued)

Today we *moved* – and how! Bags and boxes and parcels and blanket-rolls. The transport moved us down to our huts. We were really sorry to leave our house, but the huts won't be as bad as we thought. My crack that ours should be called "It's Either" has been adopted. (It's Either Too Hot or Too Cold....) We are six WDs and six WAAF together. The other two huts are entirely WAAF. There are eight beds along each side, so there's room for four more people. A shelf above the bed has one hook for coat-hangers, and the floor is covered with linoleum. Woe is me – that means polish!

There are two windows and a door at each end; the walls are concrete, with asbestos lining. No gothic architecture, this. The space around our beds is quite small, so I don't know how we'll cope with all our stuff. S/O Findlay did relieve us of stacking our bedding in our previous quarters on the day shift, but those days are gone forever. Here, we'll have to be prepared for pukka inspections daily.

The Mess on this site is a former stable – very small, but the food is better than it was on the Main Station.

Summer and winter views of Nissen huts at Blankney Hall, Digby, Lincolnshire 1944.

There's a "John" at one end of the hut, but we have to go across the Manor yard to the wash-hut, to clean up. These are the most primitive arrangements for performing ablutions. I nearly got drowned when I went over this evening to wash. It all adds to the excitement of course. There are two baths, but I foresee it'll be showers, and cold ones. The Spartan life and all that...

The business of "Ablutions" was a relatively involved procedure. First the power-house had to be notified that someone wanted to take a bath. Then once inside the bath-hut, a wave through the open window to the "Erk" – RAF parlance for an airman – at the power-house signalled that it was time for a shot of steam to be released. This condensed into water when the steam hit the tub. The trick was to get into the bathtub after the water was cool enough to avoid being scalded, but not yet ice-cold; so timing was everything.

The chief advantage of the move is that we are now living within a few hundred yards of where we work. No more leaving the house an hour before the transport leaves, in order to eat, then to catch it and ride to work. Now we can whip into the Mess and then to work immediately.

Our nice Canadian Nursing Sister has gone to a Mobile Unit in the south – leaving us lamenting. She'll be happy and will probably see some stuff. We've been too healthy to provide anything more interesting for her than the odd cold. One of the girls did break her arm when she fell off a horse, but that's about all. No palsy, leprosy, frenzy or attempted suicides to provide medical practice for poor Sister Kaines, so she left us. We didn't see much of her, but we'll miss her. She brought over a huge brown jar full of vitamin goo for us to take, during the winter. We took it, but didn't care enough for it to ask for a refill in April. The sun is out now, so we returned the empty jar today. More will be had in October.

May 7, 1944

The day we moved, we had to stick around waiting for the WAAF O.C. to inspect the house – to make sure we'd left it clean. Five minutes before the WAAF Flight Officer was due, Jamie lit a *cigar*. We all looked sort of green through the haze, when the inspecting party arrived. The WAAF Officer made no comment.

Last night we gave the WAAF their first demonstration of touch Rugby. The Sergeant caught us in the Bath-Hut just as Jamie had intercepted Helen's pass and had broken through the "line" to slide all the way down the showers for a touch-down. The Bath-Hut is lovely – a complicated system of pipes, all of which project icy water. We are quite the Spartan types now. A great shack with a cement floor, tin basins and pools of water all over the place. Ideal for water polo! I wear my rubber boots – when I remember to.

It offends the aesthetic sensibilities of the Lady who owns our estate to see wet clothes on a line outside our hut, so we have to dry 'em inside. We're hoping to have the situation rectified shortly. Someone ought to tell the Lady there's a war on. Don't know why she's allowed to live on here, anyway.

May 8th, 1944

We have been spending our free evenings cycling to various villages in the country-side. Tonight in our wanderings we stopped at a little pub, the Star and Garter, in Metheringham. We were four and when we went in some Yanks bought us a drink. I wondered whether we would be expected to devote our evening to them, after their gesture. Not a bit. They left us alone and went on with their game of darts, while we sat and watched. It wasn't till the second round that they found out we were Canadians and immediately they became hail fellow. One was from Arkansas, one from Texas, one from Michigan and the fourth from Oregon – all patients in a nearby U.S. Army Hospital, waiting to go home. I can't recall when I have enjoyed talking to strangers more.

The Texas lad had been at Dorval as a Ferry Pilot, and spent three and a half years flying in China. He's a sergeant in the Army now, and invalided due to heart. He knows Montreal pretty well, and promised to have one at the Samovar for us. Altogether a most pleasant time, and to hear American slang and a drawl did no harm.

A concession has been made re hanging out laundry. We may now put our washing on an itsy-bitsy line, until 10:30 a.m. It spoils "the view of the pawk" – so at ten-thirty, dry or not, it must come in. Here we had a Squadron-Leader, Flight-Sergeant, Flight-Officer and so on, come down to see where the ordinary ranks were hanging their thingummies. Very dignified! It's agin the law to put out washing after black-out time, for obvious reasons (the washing is obvious, that is) so I guess we get up at the crack of dawn. Nearly everyone has a cold (not I – yet) and we blame the wetness apparent in the huts. But better the Air Force should die then the old witch's "view of the pawk" be threatened. It's a grand old war!

At the last Messing meeting the WAAF representative told the Messing Officer that "The Canadians are always hungry" – which is no lie. Result: More vegetables and salads. Marvelous! We are all showing signs of renewed vim and vigour. I renewed my iron tonic last week, as well. Feel like a new person. Sleeping better, too.

As a group, we Canadian WDs were probably more out-going and at times must have seemed more like a litter of irresponsible puppies than like military personnel. Our "strange" table manners – laying down our knives at mealtimes and switching our forks from left to right hand – engendered a certain amount of teasing. As did the precious peanut butter from our parcels that we slathered on our bread with a heavy hand. Nor were we averse to hoarding bread and jam from the Mess for late night consumption as we sat huddled around the fire.

The NAAFI Canteen was another source of sustenance. Tea was a ha'penny, coffee was a penny, and cocoa was three pence and we often took turns going over with a batch of orders. Returning, laden with mugs, almost inevitably the bearer would be held to account by some weary and strung-out airwoman, who would peevishly announce, "I asked for cocoa. This is coffee." A discussion would then ensue about how – if it had cost three pence – it could be anything but cocoa. Since all three beverages, although sweet and hot, were almost indistinguishable, this made for interminable wrangles. In fact one of the unkindest curses anyone could invoke was the epithet, "May your beer turn to NAAFI tea!"

At Blankney, we falsely assumed that as Spring wore on and gardens were producing, we might occasionally have salads, something we sorely missed; but such luxuries were hard to come by for anyone. We did, however, discover that Lady Londesborough's gardener was not above selling us lettuce and tomatoes from her green-house, so we took it in turn to purchase these treasures for our group in the Mess. Once in a while we were also able to procure eggs from local farmers, and this was always an occasion for rejoicing.

We're not as frantically busy as we have been, but expect little leisure time once things start rolling along. I don't know whether to hope we have another month like April or not. We'll have it anyway, so my hoping won't affect it one way or another. We expect lots in return, though, so the peace of the country-side these lovely summer nights will be marred again. But not seriously, we hope. And not for long. Should be an exciting time.

May 10th, 1944

The problem of "Where We Are to Hang our Laundry" has not yet been solved. This morning we deliberately washed our largest articles and strung 'em up in the hut, so that the Inspecting Party had to flap in and out among lines of wet clothes. I resurrected my blue (ski) underwear for the occasion. It was lying, clean, at the bottom of my kit-bag, but I washed it anyway and it's been dripping ever since. Even this letter is wet. Perhaps now we'll get a line outdoors. The problem is what to do now that we've spitefully done the washing, had the Inspection, and are left with everything wet!

Group Captain McNab, our C.O., is a Canadian. He is young, has ideas and he's very easy to talk to. Was one of twenty-four who were the first RCAF Squadron in the Battle of Britain. I believe he was the first Canadian to shoot down an enemy aircraft in the war. Only four of that Squadron are alive.

S/O Findlay has given me a couple of reports to write up for the Personal Relations Section in London. They need material – apparently – and want to see what kind of stuff can be turned out. It's interesting work and I can do it in odd minutes. I'm enthused at the idea.

We are shocking everybody by putting chocolate sauce from home on our desserts. Here they swamp everything with custard – fruit, pudding, cake... It makes me never want to see custard sauce again. There's just no accounting for tastes.

We are able to borrow bikes from the Air Force. Still find the Rule of the Road here funny/odd and am about to break my neck with English brakes.

May 17, 1944

Much has been written about comradeship. Some of it tripe. You have to be in a few tight corners to find out for yourself what honest-to-goodness comradeship is. Here, it's living with the salt-of-the-earth type of WD that is in our hut, sharing everything and dividing the work, helping each other over the rougher spots. It's the kind of thing you don't talk about, but one can't help being conscious of it.

Odd, I've heard men say (and I'm afraid I've heard women say it, too) that with all the qualities with which the female sex in endowed, loyalty is not one of them. You'll never get me to believe that or agree with it. Give women the kind of leader that deserves their loyalty and she'll have it – with a wholesome respect and a heck of a lot of affection thrown in. I am thinking of our own Section Officer, who is a rose among some of the thorns here.

Bit by bit, we're achieving something. Whether the war will last long enough (or whether we will!) to see a Brave New World on our camp, I don't know.

A new feather in our cap. The WAAF have invited our shift to go down to the Main Camp to give the girls a gen-lecture on Canada. Not about climate and the Chinook winds and the number of bushels of wheat exported; but from the point of view of English girls going out to Canada, either married to Canadians, or as emigrants. What they can expect to find. The differences in money, postage, food, transportation – all the things which, conversely, we found (and are finding) so strange here. It's a compliment they've paid us, and we hope our evening is a success for them.

The Education Officer gave us a stack of reference books, and Jamie and I cycled down to camp last night to get some more from S/O Findlay. We three perused books until we all got so homesick that we changed the subject and talked of something else! (I'm sure the idea that the world is flat originated in the head of the first caveman who lived in Lincolnshire. I get the feeling myself sometimes, that I'm going to fall off!) There were pictures in the books of the

Gaspé, the Laurentians, the St. Lawrence, the Maritimes, and good old Algonquin Park. If I could only see even a little hill or a river that runs swiftly enough not to be mistaken for artificial irrigation!

We go to bed in broad daylight. At 10:45 it's still light. The birds are asleep, but the lambs bleat away – a lovely pastoral scene! No eggs from the Heckled Hens yet, but we're trying! If they'd only come in and lay one little egg in the hut – but they won't.

Have never seen so many kinds of wild flowers nor in such profusion. Our hut is a continual ever-changing mass of scent and blossom. The lilacs are at their best just now. Wild almond is finished and, until this week, the apple blossoms were heavenly.

May 22nd, 1944

I suppose it's useless to ask you not to listen to every news broadcast, once things begin to hum; but it's not going to be a pretty story for the first little while. We went through a vicarious Hell in 1940 and 1941, reading the papers and listening to the radio. I am unable to spare you that sort of thing, but our one comfort is that the Arch of Victory Churchill spoke of is before us. We, over here, will probably be too concerned with our work to use our imaginations, or even to read the war correspondents' realistic stories of the hospital-trains. In that way, we are lucky. Unless the Germans give in suddenly – and they won't – it's going to be the fiercest battle on land, sea and in the air that the world has ever seen. The Huns know they're fighting for their lives now. And preparations on both sides are, I am certain, beyond anything we expected even a year ago.

Any camera film #120 or #620 to be had? There is none here. I don't imagine there is much chance of any at home either. Our supply is just about petering out.

May 25th, 1944

Back from a "36" in the sunny South. Able to say that I saw summer once in England, anyway. The new train-cuts are disastrous, and had it not been that I was reluctant not to accomplish what I'd set out to do (get to Basingstoke) and see Padre Grant Hollingworth, I would have stayed in Lincoln.

Sev, [*Nellie Severson Gibson*] the newest Canadian bride, was going down to London to meet her husband. We hopped an RCAF truck to Lincoln and of course there was no two o'clock train. Sev *had* to get to London and I wanted to, so we went to the Corporation Limits by bus. An army truck took us to Newark and we stepped out of it into an Air Force petrol truck, so six o'clock found us in the heart of London. Who said, "It's Quicker By Rail"?

First RCAF wedding held at Blankney Church. Nellie Severson and Jack Gibson, March 25, 1944.

By bus and tube I reached Waterloo Station and hopped on a train to Basingstoke just as it was pulling out. Grant met me at the station there at eight thirty. Took me to dinner at the same pub (the only one) as in December, and I tucked away a huge meal while we both talked at once. We left my knapsack at the house where I was to stay and walked over the grounds of the Hospital. It's light now until after ten-thirty and though I had seen the grounds and the Hospital in December, May is the month. Warm, pleasant evenings and the English country-side, woods and fields simply heavenly.

The people I stayed with overnight were some friends of Grant's – a very kind elderly couple who make a practice of taking in Service people and making them feel at home. They had had two American lads staying with them last week-end and their imitations of an American drawl were priceless.

I had bacon and two eggs for breakfast – worthy of note. Grant took me up to the Hospital then to see some of the handicraft work the patients have been doing and we went over to a Parade Square to watch a coloured American Battalion drilling.

The idea now, in catching a train, is to go to the station and wait until one comes -which is what we did. We only had to wait about half an hour. I was back in "Blighty" by one o'clock, went to the Strand Palace for some lunch and became involved in a most interesting discussion with a lady at the next table. We exchanged views on the strikes, equal pay for women, education here and abroad, Churchill, food, transportation, the British aristocracy. The stranger was a person of broad and tolerant thought and I learned a lot from her explanations of some of the things we talked about. When I got up to go, she asked me my name and said hers was Clive. I am still wondering what she thought of this Canadian's comments on the aristocracy! [*I later learned that her husband was Lieut.-Gen. Sir George Sidney Clive.*]

I went at once to King's Cross Station to check on trains. Found that the only one left at six p.m. so I had a couple of hours to put in. Went by bus back to Trafalgar Square, took a couple of snaps and walked around a bit. Then down the Strand past the Church of St. Clements' Dane (Oranges and Lemons, the Bells of....) which is now just a skeleton of stone. It bears a sign listing the names of many who once lived in the parish – Old Dr. Johnson is one. Then on into Fleet Street. Probably I enjoy this walk most because it's the first walk I took in London. St. Paul's Dome is visible all the way down and the sun shone on it in a most dazzling way.

The train was packed, but I was early enough to get a seat. The trip north from London by train is not very interesting. Not to be compared with the same trip the day before, when we followed the main road in our truck. I slept most of the way up to Grantham, where I had to change. Sev was on the same train, farther up, so we joined forces at Grantham. Had a bit of time before our other train was due in. We were wondering what to do and whether to look for some supper – it was then eight o'clock – when we came upon a little R.C. chapel. Sev examined the tomb-stones outside and I went in. I lit a candle and thought of you.

We were in Lincoln by 9:30 and caught the 10:15 bus back to camp. We'll be back on the Graveyard in a few days – the 24th, to be exact. Far from dreading it, we are quite bucked at the thought. Far happier, really, when we are cracking at the work and no one has time to care whether we're Canadian or not. The work has to be done then and there isn't time to worry about who does it! It's the busiest time and somehow we wish we could always work on that shift. Silly, because we wouldn't be able to hold out for long.

May 27, 1944

Germany is indeed being rocked to its foundations. Just a while longer and if we can hold on, it will be finished. The last pull is always the hardest and everyone is impatient now. But the Japanese will get his, too. Things are at last going all our way and Rome itself will soon be in our hands, we hope.

We're in a mild flap about our proposed Canada Night next Wednesday. Miss Findlay is a wizard at producing anything we ask for, but even she, the Intelligence Officer, has no map of Canada. She's trying to rake one up.

We plan to have coffee and biscuits after the talk. All has to be arranged yet and this is the week we work four shifts in a little more than two days. To make things worse, S/O Findlay may be going to London on business any day, so we're all keeping our fingers crossed it won't be until after Wednesday.

The following week I'm to go down to a nearby village to talk to the girls' club on the same subject. They want a Canadian Airwoman, so I'm it. Hope I don't bore the poor things stiff. The Education Officer is to censor my outline, so likely he'll have something to say about my approach. The way I see it, what people want is an exchange of ideas and a slant on our customs. Anyone can get statistics out of a book.

May 29, 1944

We have been able to buy bottles of Lemon Extract. It's concentrated lemon juice, to be precise. Not the kind you read about people getting drunk on – unfortunately! It's good with water, and the WAAF showed us how to mix it with beer in the Canteen. You can hardly taste the lemon, but it does wonders for the beer. The nearest thing to a Coke that we'll see this summer!

Am reading as much as time allows – the history of the district, Canadian books, material in connection with our work. It passes the time. The movies shown on camp are light comedy, usually, and provide relaxation and a laugh.

May 31st,1944

Went down to Digby on my bike today to see the person in charge of the Girls' Club at which I am to strut my stuff. Found her to be a member of a most charming family – farmers, living in an old stone house with a thatched roof and a magnificent garden. The young lady, Miss Gibson, teaches school and practically has her Pilot's license. Has very Bolshy ideas, too. When I set out, I was almost overpowered by shyness and it took everything I had to keep on going and not ride back and tell Miss Findlay I'd changed my mind, but in the end they turned out to be dears – the whole family.

June 3rd, 1944

The Canada evening was a lot of fun. Jamie was superb, and the others were very good as well. After the coffee and biscuits, we had a short film on Canada. Nostalgia! We steered clear of making comparisons and simply tried to give an honest picture of what it means to be a Canadian. My soap-box was Education and of course I forgot my notes! How unlike me?

Jamie remarked that she thought English people going out to Canada would find it lonely, because Canada is a lonely country – the scenery being wild, and so on. "But," she said, "you will find sympathy there. Canadians know what it is to be lonely, even in a big city, especially in the winter". Several

WAAF came up to us afterwards and said they were conscience-stricken that we had been on the camp for so long and they had done nothing and said nothing to make us feel that we belonged. Jamie hadn't meant to make a pointed remark, but having kept us in the refrigerator for five months, the girls have decided to take us off the ice, and to thaw out.

With the arrival of warmer weather in that Spring of 1944, in the interests of ridding ourselves of our winter pallor, we developed the habit of retreating to the H.Q's rooftop during off-duty hours to indulge in a bit of sunbathing. This practice happily continued until a message from Group Captain McNab appeared in the Daily Routine Orders.

Corporal Jean " Jamie" Jamieson at Digby, Lincolnshire, 1944.

Collection of M. Jean Houston

You would love the new orders recently posted by our O.C. It has been brought to his attention that personnel have been sun-bathing – nude – on the roof, and while it is not his intention to advise us upon the question of decency and morality involved... we must be aware of the menace to life, due to the fact that pilots are indulging in the low-flying of their aircraft. So the roof is out of bounds, now, – dressed or undressed – and we have a new slogan – "We Serve That Men May Fly... Low ".

R.C.A.F. Overseas
June 6th, 1944

I wish I could tell you what it has been like on the Graveyard Shift of late. I got to bed at five this morning and at six we all listened to the German news broadcast suggesting that D-Day had come. The official British report came some hours later. You in North America will have awakened on the morning of June the sixth, 1944, to hear the momentous news. I wonder what the reaction is over there. There is a tenseness here, combined with a relief that we need no longer wonder "when". We have had three hours' sleep since Sunday morning and are standing by in case we are called.

When orders came out early in April that no one would be granted Leave aside from specific exceptions such as air crew, we knew that D-Day was imminent, although no one had any idea when it would arrive. The Allied Forces had been softening up the Continent and – depending on the weather – we, in Ops, continued to be busy. April passed into May and by early June there was a high state of tension on all fronts, as one day faded into the next. We later heard that D-Day had been planned for the fifth of June, but that the weather had made it seem wise to postpone it until the sixth.

Our shift went on duty at midnight on the fifth. With Double Daylight Time it remained light until very late in the evening in the north of England. As we went for our-pre-shift meal, the sky was black with planes. We later heard that there were around twelve thousand aircraft aloft that night – all heading in the same direction. We were prepared to be busy in the Ops Room, and our expectations were more than realized.

With the entire shift on duty, we were able to relieve each other at ten minute intervals, but no one even dozed during those periods of respite. We simply couldn't risk going back to work half-awake. Some of us were sent off duty at 5 a.m., since most of our own aircraft had returned by that time. We trudged over to the Mess and then back to our Nissen huts, where we fell on our cots without even bothering to wash, while a few listened to the news on the radio.

About nine o'clock, an excited WAAF arrived at our door announcing that D-Day had begun. This hardly came as a surprise to the occupants, who'd been awakened from a deep sleep, and she was greeted with a few uncharitable remarks before we all rolled over and fell fast asleep for another few hours.

June 8th, 1944
4 a.m.

Wot a day! Wot a day! They do seem to be good at thinking up things to keep us from sleeping when we're working Graveyard and are supposed to be in bed during the day. This afternoon we had to cycle down to camp. The dentist overhauled us, – all the WDs – and then we went around to the M.O. and had to undergo two injections – Tetanus and T.A.B.T. – our annual dose.

Got back to camp in time for tea, and then off to a village five miles from here, – once more on my bike.

There were about twenty village girls at the Canada meeting, ranging in age from twelve to seventeen. Also four or five adults. Before I launched forth on my subject, we drank the inevitable cup of tea. The girls were interested in everything from Hopscotch to Unemployment Insurance and we ended up

Canadian WDs at the 'Horse and Jockey', Waddington, Lincolnshire, June 1944. S/O Grace Findlay (centre) receiving a "send off" prior to leaving for a London posting.

simply having an informal discussion on all sorts of things. I learned lots, and I suppose the girls absorbed a bit, too.

Cycled back at ten-fifteen, across the Lincolnshire fields and out on to the highway. Clouded sky, but blue showing through, and a heavenly sunset.

Am glad the evening is behind me. Have scarcely had time to think about it, other than to recall that I had no chance to do any preparation and to wonder how I'd manage to get through.

The previous evening, in between a dozen little duties, such as sitting in the Guard Room for a couple of hours (Duty Stooge, they call it), booking people in and out, I had a report to write for S/O Findlay – a write-up of the outcome of the baseball series, an account of a birthday party we had, details of our Canada night last week. I sat listening to the King's broadcast and as I stubbed out cigarettes, thought how crazy it was to be occupied writing this, when the papers are publishing extra editions and the radio blares forth news of world-importance.

Then it occurred to me that these very things – a baseball game, a birthday party, the privilege of talking about one's country without fear for one's life – are the very things that are being fought for. It's the awful feeling that we get sometimes, that nothing matters. It goes away again, with the realization that everything matters. I had it at the time of Hong Kong and Dieppe and during the months of the desert-battle.

Thursday afternoon we had to cycle to camp to have the usual routine check up of our gas equipment. We were all too weary, by evening, to make any decisions for ourselves, so instead of trying to sleep, we followed the crowd to Lincoln to a "Canada" dance at the Assembly Rooms there. I had made up my mind that I'd enjoy myself or else – having made the effort to go to the dance. Ran into three F/O's who had been on the boat with us. They took me out for a beer, I met their crews and we all went back to the dance together. We had to get back to be on duty at midnight, so we left the dance far too early.

Yesterday we had to hang around for Pay-Parade and only the thought of some cash kept us awake. By evening we were set up again and went down to a Canada dance on our camp. A super band from London (RCAF) is in the district and it's worth going a long way to hear. Met a very nice YMCA Education and Allied Services man and spent most of the evening with him. Discussed the power of the Church most of the time we were dancing!

The Group Captain spoke to us at one point. He has a super remedy for injections. He recommends several straight whiskies and then bed. Says that when you wake up you don't know whether it's the injections or the hang-over.

Have been amusing ourselves just now, trying to sketch. One of the WAAF is quite good and has been encouraging us to try. You know me – I can't even draw a doughnut, let alone anything devious, like an egg. But we've had fun drawing everything in sight – the huts, the trees, the hedge, the hens, each other and the Sergeant. And the WAAF has been examining the results with a serious eye! Am afraid I'll never quite qualify for the Group of Seven, somehow.

The grounds and English country-side can't hold a candle to the campus [*at Ste. Anne de Bellevue*] but they're certainly trying. The wild poppies are ablaze in the fields. I like them better than most other flowers – no perfume, but such colour. If opium-eaters recapture in December some of the rapture of live poppies in June, I don't blame them. And when I wear a poppy on the 11th of November, it will be not only because of Flanders' Fields, but because of the long, long thoughts some of us had once, in Lincolnshire's pleasant fields. The pink horse-chestnut (unfamiliar to us Canadians) is over, but the climbing roses are at the window and the gardens are a mass of colour.

It's a thrill to watch the bombers racing to meet and then go off to the attack. They look like dogs with their ears back, in pursuit of a rabbit. You can almost feel the exhilaration. The Hun is getting what he has been promising Britain for years.

June 18, 1944

The pilot-less plane [*often referred to as a "doodle bug"*] is keeping us from thinking of much else – on duty, that is. You probably hear about it in the news-casts and see stuff in the papers.

June 27, 1944

This week our spirits have alternately soared to the heights and hit a new low. It was quite a coincidence, we thought, that a lot of new orders came out the day after S/O Findlay left; however we've got used to that idea – after awhile. On our day off, last Friday, nine of us went on a picnic. Took our new Officer, (S/O Annette Schalburg) along and had a whale of a time. It was a glorious June day. Being an organized party (the official term), we were able to wear slacks and sports shirts, and we rode our bikes up inclines and coasted down slopes with sheer delight at the thought of being free for awhile. We had a wonderful tea beside a pool.

We stopped at a pub to get one for the road, and the pub-keeper brought out snaps of all the RCAF boys he's had billetted with him at various times. Insisted we have a drink on the house. The first WDs he's seen etc. etc. We got back to camp about ten – saddle-sore is the word – but very happy.

The next day we had a "pukka" inspection. Lots of WAAF Officers and our own WD Officer. Buch, running true to form, put up lots of wet, drippy washing at her end of the hut. Someone must have put a flea in S/O Schalburg's ear. She played up beautifully. Raised the devil because we had washing in the hut, and I wish you could have seen her face when she heard *why* we couldn't put it outside. She issued a few ultimatums around the place and gave them three days to figure out a way to get our mail to the Post Office a bit quicker. (It lies around for days.) But about the washing I fear she can do little. However, it's fun trying.

I came down here to another RAF camp yesterday with a WD Corporal for a week's course – Radar. Seems a bit futile, if we aren't staying in the work, but it's the course I've been pleading for for months. And now, thanks to S/O Findlay, we've got here at last. Very interesting and the camp itself is a splendid one. Very friendly. A hail-fellow, come-on-in-and-sit-down atmosphere. Very few rules, lots of freedom and our spare time is our own. Also, the girls have been extremely good to us.

Fran (the Corporal) and I have a "24" tomorrow and we're going in to Peterborough for the occasion. We thought of going to London, but it's a good place to stay away from if one has only 24 hours.

The trip down here involved a three-hour bus ride – (changing buses twice) on Monday morning. It was hard to believe that we had only come thirty-five miles. The atmosphere here is friendly. We are thoroughly enjoying the camp, the work and our spare time. The food is an improvement and there's fresh milk! The WAAF ordered a pint a day for us from the milk-man, so we are enjoying our first regular milk in England. I had forgotten how much I missed it. To have a whole pint to myself is wonderful.

Yesterday Fran and I went in to the YW at Peterborough. There's a brand-new Hostel for Service girls there. It's a most pleasant place – bright, fresh paint, comfortable furniture and lots of hot water. We put our knap-sacks on our beds and had some tea and a bun before we set out to see the town. We shopped around for a couple of hours. Bought a box of strawberries each (the first we've seen this year – price 2/10) and a bunch of carrots. We hadn't had time to drink our milk, so we'd brought it to town with us -the makings of a meal! We were able to get tickets for the Court Players' production of Noel Coward's *Hay-Fever* and then off we went to dinner.

We had a very good meal at a hotel called the Angel and the other person at our table was a French woman. She could hardly speak English and practically had tears of joy in her eyes when I spoke French. The outcome was that she called for wine, wishing to celebrate in the true French manner. They brought us some Algerian red wine and from then on it was "Vive la France," "toujours gai", "come-on-and-be-merry." We talked of De Gaulle, post-war prospects and all the rest. Our new acquaintance has been over here since France fell. Her husband is in the French Cabinet, wandering around North Africa probably. She was one of those interesting people one runs across, here and there.

We set off for the play, Fran and I, at 8:15. Our seats were good and we were feeling rather in tune with the world. It was the play that fell down – corny is the word – but we laughed a lot so our money wasn't wasted, by a long shot.

When we got back to the YW, we found the place had been taken by storm by dozens of WAAF. One is married to an Australian, another is engaged to a Canadian, a third is a Polish-Jewess and so on. All types, all different. We talked until about one a.m. and ate strawberries!

We spent a lazy morning today and caught the noon bus back to our quarters. We're on duty until five p.m. and on again at midnight.

Fran and I hope to go to Peterborough again on Saturday. We're due back at our own Station Sunday night, and if we pull the right strings, we ought to be able to have another overnight pass on our way. Two Yanks stationed near here have asked us to go out, and I want another tour of the Cathedral before we leave for the flatlands.

Just before we left on Monday, enough WAAF arrived to replace all the

WDs. We hope this is a good sign. Anything that points that way is optimistic for us. But we haven't actually heard that they are meant to replace us.

We went to the train to see S/O Findlay off ten days ago. With her in the compartment were two M.O's – Squadron Leaders who had been torpedoed on their way to France and had to come back to be re-kitted. They had lots to say and we found ourselves envying Miss Findlay her journey.

The WAAF had a fifth Birthday this week, so we had specially good meals for the occasion. The NCO's waited on us at the table and the Officers served the NCO's. There was a party in the Mess that evening. Fran and I were in Peterborough, so we didn't go, but I gather it was a brawl. In spite of the way things are progressing on the Continent, the WAAF will likely have another birthday or two. Our Air Marshal, Sir Roderick Hill, has just announced that WAAF may go to France. We are hoping against hope (and in vain) that we may get there, but it's pretty doubtful.

It's certainly good to get away and see how the wheels go around in another camp. I'm glad we've had this week down here – if only to see that a Station needn't be all discipline and orders.

South-west view of Lincoln Cathedral.

July 6th, 1944
Digby

Things have piled up. Casualties are less than had been expected, as you know, but we seem to have been having a run of bad luck with our friends in the vicinity. Two of the lads Helen and I were going to a dance with last night were Missing yesterday. I don't think one can ever become hardened to this sort of thing – seeing the same people day after day, and then having the ranks depleted. We went over to a nearby U.S.A. Hospital the evening of the Fourth of July to visit some of the lads there. Just back from France and what a scene! They're getting wonderful care and seem cheery about it. Anxious to get back and give the Hun another sock. But I'm afraid some of them are grounded for good. One paratrooper had jumped in North Africa, Sicily and now France. Some of their stories were dramatic; others had tales to tell that would give anyone the shivers. We said we'd go again some evening soon and write some letters home for some of them.

Last night four of us went with S/O Schalburg to Lincoln Cathedral to hear Haydn's "Creation". Very beautiful. We had fish and chips afterwards at the Overseas Club, and a heated discussion about whether military training ought to be compulsory for youth after the war. It's a subject that will take a lot of thought.

July 9th, 1944

The new tenseness is affecting everyone in various ways. I've watched one of my best friends go off and get drunk when she heard that yet another of our lads is Missing. And I've watched our officers get more and more wrought-up, with the result that their grip on us has tightened, with a corresponding effect on the ranks. When people lose all responsibility for their own individual actions, they lose their sense of disinterested morality. It's vicious circle. On the other side of the ledger, there's the marvel that our own WD Officer has enough perspicacity to size up the situation and act accordingly. She's kidded us along until we got a tennis tournament organized and a new baseball series on the go. We're going to practice square-dancing next week. It all adds to the fun.

I wasn't able to tell you this one until I was safely back on our own camp, but one night on our course at Peterborough, we were told to turn in because there'd be nothing doing that night. We tramped off to the Rest Hut, and were nicely settled in bed, when the 'phone rang. The two Canadians would report for duty at once.

So Fran and I climbed back into our uniforms and set out across the fields. We were talking as we went, when first thing we knew, someone said, "Halt! Who goes there?" It didn't occur to me that the sentry wouldn't recognize us, but since we were strangers, naturally he didn't. All our own sentries know us and rarely are we even asked for a Pass. With a great big grin, I said "Friend" and kept on walking. A cold steel bayonet barely an inch from my eyes made me change my mind. A few explanations and we were allowed to pass on, but I was considerably subdued, I must say!

Fran and I went to a short service at the Peterborough Cathedral last Saturday afternoon. The little choir boys wear pale blue cassocks and their angelic faces belie their impish tricks, I suspect. We saw the tomb of Catherine of Aragon and the spot where Mary Queen of Scots was dug up – upon the order of her son. All very cosy. Afterwards we bought some more strawberries and went to the RCAF H.Q. to see our Canadian friends. Went back to the YWCA for tea and there we met a girl from Montreal High whom I hadn't seen since school. We completed the evening by having a beer with some Yanks bent on celebrating the 4th of July or Dominion Day or any day. Caught the last bus back to camp just in time to go on duty.

Today Larry, our YMCA Supervisor, came down on a truck which was loaded with pillows and gay patch-work quilts – gifts of the Canadian Red Cross. So now we each have a pillow and a quilt and the hut is much cheerier. The WAAF O.C. made a crack yesterday, when one of our N.C.O.'s made a sensible suggestion. She said, "Ask your WD outfit. They might supply a red plush carpet". Then today came the quilts and pillows to soften our blows and we feel just a little bit like sticking out our tongues! Anyway, I'm thankful to have a pillow. It's not exactly a "fevver" one, but a great big improvement on the bolster which has been mine. You see what small things make us happy. Not that a pillow or the lack of one matters a damn in this war-torn world.

July 12, 1944

We've won the battle of the washing. It sapped all our energy doing it, but we are victorious, if exhausted. It was worth it to go to all the trouble of putting up wet clothes. The Senior Medical Officer from H.Q. arrived this week, unheralded and unsung. He raised absolute hell when he inspected the huts. He stormed about, raving that it was all very unhealthy and so on. So Lady So-and-so has to bear up with "the view from the Pawk" being spoiled and we approve of the order that appeared, saying all laundry will in future be put outside. If the WAAF Officers had wanted to do anything about it, they could have asked the S.M.O. ages ago to come and put his foot down – but no. The whole thing is so silly. The clothes-line is in a forest, and can't even be seen.

We're on the Graveyard again. Jamie and I are among those with a special job which involves working until two or three, curling up on a very hard table for some shut-eye and answering the phone – perhaps at 4:00 a.m. – to work again. A little while ago the 'phone rang and Jamie made a dash for it in the dark, while I fought with the black-out curtains so we could put on the lights. Someone else (talking in her sleep) pleaded, "Oh, don't jump out the window – oh, please don't!" so we had to waken her to get her to go back to sleep properly. A most efficient crew, as you can see! Considering that the "drop" from the window is three feet, into a flower-bed, no one's life was seriously endangered.

July 15, 1944

Have just completed a day's trip to Sheffield and back. One of the WAAF was married today and Jamie and I wanted to be there, so we came off duty at eight a.m. and snuck off. We hitched from here to Lincoln and to Newark, via Worksop. We finally got to Sheffield just on the stroke of two. It was a pretty wedding and the reception afterwards was fun. Oh, I do like Yorkshire people! In every instance, at every opportunity, they open their hearts to us and those of the WAAF who have been friendly towards us have – almost without exception – been those from Yorkshire.

July 23, 1944

You recall Mark Twain's remark that Puget Sound enjoyed more beautiful winter weather all summer than any place he had ever visited. That must have been before he came to England.

July 27th, 1944

Jamie and I snuck off at eight o'clock on Monday. From Newark we got a ride in a 15 cwt. truck with a Major in the paratroops and his driver. Their bed-rolls were in the back of the truck, so we were well set-up and we think it's a wonderful way to see the country. We were in York by one o'clock – slightly green from the speed and the curves in the road, but very happy. The Major drove us right to the hotel and offered to drive us back the next day.

He was at the door on the dot of 11:30 a.m. and we stopped twice on the road for tea and a bun, because he was concerned lest we find the trip too much. He came miles out of his way to bring us right to the camp gate. We were there by four and on duty at five. We were amused that he made the driver seek out all the straight roads so we wouldn't have to go around corners!

July 31, 1944

So the war goes on. Things we read and things we are told, all point one way. It's getting pretty tense in Berlin, one would think. Maybe soon, yes? Let us hope!

Am working in the Intelligence Branch (HQ. Digby) now. Life is new and different. Looks as though when the remustering takes place, this will be mine. Am loving it. Cycling down to camp at eight in morning and back at six in the evening with an hour for lunch, which I have at camp.

> *The main functions of this Intelligence work involved processing, mounting or filing in-coming information and keeping wall maps of the Continent up to date. This included up-to-the-hour messages about the enemy's coastal defences, so the pilots would know what to expect.*

August 7th, 1944

Things are going ahead so *fast* that they're running right off our maps and we have to make continual adjustments. Can't make me mad that way, though!

"The Hairy Chop" – Mary Buch with Intelligence and Met Officers, RCAF, Digby HQ., Lincolnshire. Summer 1944.

Canadian Forces Photographic Unit, DND -PL41822

Some members of RCAF 411 Squadron, Digby, Lincolnshire.

Aug. 19th, 1944

The situation here goes on apace. It is now sure that we pull out of here at the end of the month. My heart is torn between Yorkshire and London, for a variety of reasons. Yorkshire I love – and Mona and many of our friends are there – yet, for us all, London holds enchantment which need not be referred to here!

August 21st, 1944

The inner gap has been closed and our boys roll along. These are the days when one tends to become impatient with the Germans for their unwillingness to see what seems to us so obvious. The past month has seen great leaps and bounds. Pray that the next two or three will see as much progress made and the filthy job on the Continent finished.

I have been packing, by fits and starts. No packing I've ever done has given me quite so much pleasure! Yesterday I had the morning off and really enjoyed sleeping in. A wet, soggy morning – obviously meant to be spent just so. Other than the two mornings I've had in York, when we got up at nine-thirty, it's the first time for about five weeks that I haven't had to be up and polished and out, so it was a great occasion. Too bad I wasn't awake to enjoy it. Or am I getting a little mixed up?

Inspection by King George VI at RCAF Fighter Station #1, Digby, Lincolnshire. Summer 1944.

In the late 1960s, twenty-five years after World War II, while visiting with cousins in England, we went by car on a day's jaunt which included revisiting Lincoln Cathedral, and also made a slight detour to the site of what had once been Blankney Hall. A fire a few years prior to our visit had devastated the entire manor house. It was no more. The Nissen huts and some of the out-buildings were still there, but the grass had grown up in front of the doors and there were old mattresses hanging out the windows. Otherwise no trace remained of the young Canadians who had once lived and worked there all those years ago, and I felt a twinge of regret at having come back. I should have remembered Walt Whitman's words of caution, "Never return to the worn doorsill" ....

PART EIGHT

From Pillar to Post
September 1944 – July 1945

(New address)
No. 62 Base, R.C.A.F
Overseas Sept. 3rd, 1944
[Linton, Yorkshire]

Have at last moved. To go back a bit; a few days before we left our previous post, we went down to Peterborough to play baseball with a WAAF team. We had a wonderful day, with lunch at the American Forces' Club. We lost the game but it was a good one. Had an amusing experience afterwards. Got back to the YWCA to change, and I found myself holding an Airman's knap-sack. I was without clothes until H.Q. got cracking and recovered mine! Why do things like that always happen to *me?*

There was a dance afterwards. They'd had tea for us first and we came back in a transport in the wee small hours.

The other sixteen have been posted to London. We (four of us, including Helen) came here. It's been like coming home (almost!) as Paddy and seven others that we knew from Dartmouth, N.S. are all here. The Officer who brought our draft over is Officer Commanding of the WDs. There are many, many whom we knew either in Canada or in Bournemouth. WDs have only been stationed here since January, so we are among the veterans. One girl asked me if I had just arrived. Thinking she meant at the Base, I said, "Yes". "Oh well," she said, "you'll soon get to know the ropes in England – I' ve been here seven days".

Most of the Clerks have just recently been brought over. We are told that people at home are not to send us any Christmas parcels. If that's true, it's a fine thing. We don't want to come home yet and that's the implication.

We were all set to go to the Continent until ten days ago, when H.Q. decided that there was no place for us in our work. I guess they're right, though I hate to admit it!

Sgts. Margot Norum (left) and Pat "Paddy" Seccombe (right) at Linton-on-Ouse, Yorkshire with tandem bicycle.

Helen and I are sharing a large upstairs room. The other two are downstairs. The house is really a beaut! Much nicer than our previous equivalent. There is more room and brighter, cleaner paint. The plumbing facilities, including a decent bath, are upstairs. Quite a change! No more scraping of shins and elbows when scrubbing.

This is a dandy place for entertainment, with plenty of sports and books. Helen has been made Queen of the Education Office and already has catalogued half the books, planned a new type of music programme, revised courses, etc. This chicken is in the I.O. (Intelligence Office) and loving it. The only catch is that we're on that grim shift – twenty-four hours on, twenty-four off. The day starts at 8:00 a.m. One goes to work and one stays!

Sept. 11th, 1944.

The food is good here. The Canadians aren't necessarily the best cooks in the world, but they certainly have a knack of making uninteresting food at least palatable. And it was pretty grim before, so you'll be glad to hear that things have improved. We watched the boys' ball-game yesterday afternoon – or rather, we attended the game. Lay on blankets on the field and counted 'planes as they raced across the sky. The element of *wonder* about flying is never absent from my mind. I could watch forever.

The crews are superstitious. It is an accepted thing – for one thing – that when they walk out of the office to get into their kites, no girls follow them out. It brings bad luck. Nor does one say good-bye ... *ever*! It's "See you later" or "So long". The boys also don't like any women to hang around the kites. They take a dim view of it. None of the WDs working around here have time, but once in awhile someone from a nearby station comes over who doesn't *know*....

There's a certain type of equipment occasionally issued to the Boys, and when they see it they wince. [*This was a small celluloid- encased packet with a cord attached which was worn around a flier's neck if he was part of the crew of a Lancaster bomber. Inside the packet was an armband bearing the Union Jack and some Russian script. In the event that they came down in Russian-held territory, the armband was intended to provide instant proof that this was a friend rather than a foe. When the crews were issued these packets, they knew at once that the target lay so far inside Germany that there would be a point of no return if they ran into trouble.*] The old superstition about things happening in threes still hangs around, as well. I wonder why we let ourselves think about these things? I'm not superstitious (I keep telling myself!) yet I find myself watching for these stupid things. Gremlins are more than a myth. Even the King believes in *them*! He said so in a radio broadcast.

Paddy is still getting into dreadful scrapes – without meaning to. Not very long ago she was on night duty and everything closed down at four a.m. She tidied up the office, dumped the ash-trays and lay down on the floor to sleep, after locking the door. The waste basket caught fire due to the butts, and she slept blissfully on. Then, the table went up in flames and the smoke attracted the attention of someone in the hangars. They had to crawl through a window to get her out. She was quite unruffled and apparently oblivious to the danger of it all.

Sept. 13th, 1944

Was that business at Caen necessary? I'm afraid it probably was – as much as any of this bloodshed is. We would never have gotten so far without it. But the price of it all! [*On July 25, 1944, the Canadians had been in a fierce battle at Caen-St. André, and the Black Watch was decimated. Major Phil Griffin, a Macdonald College graduate, whom Marion Strang and I had both known, was among those killed.*] There aren't many of the original Battalion left now. The only philosophy that keeps us sane here, watching our crews go out and not come back, is that whatever they find "Out There" must be better than what they've left behind.

News from the Boys has been very encouraging. September 5th was the latest. They had had the pleasure of marching through Dieppe, which they had been looking forward to.

We miss the Canadian autumn. There is nothing like it here, although harvest-time in England has a beauty all its own.

By early August 1944, Allied bombers had begun heavy attacks on the launching sites from which the enemy's V-1 rockets were being fired, and by the end of that month our Linton Squadrons 408 and 426 were also targetting German aerodromes in France, Belgium and the Netherlands. September saw greater Allied concentration on LeHavre and the Ruhr.

Sept. 27th, 1944

Am in London. It's the tail end (or perhaps the tale?) of my Leave, and what a wonderful time it has been, all told. I had a day in Manchester on the 19th and went to a play – *Junior Miss* – with S/O Schalburg. Then went on to North Wales the following day. I stayed there with the cousins until Saturday, and have been here in London ever since. Tomorrow I set out to go back to York.

Much of my time was spent in trying to find out what happened to my brother, Chris. I finally did find out. He's still in a British hospital in France – or was. (He may be back here by now...) Shrapnel in the calf of one leg, and apparently not serious. Also he has a superficial hand-wound. Am much relieved that it is not worse.

Feel a different person for the change, the rest and the superb beauty of the scenery in Wales. My English cousins ran me ragged cycling, climbing mountains and so on, but the "sturdy Canadian" enjoyed every bit of it – and wants to go back.

London in September is the best ever. I could bear more of this life and wish I could thumb my nose at the Air Force for a while longer! However, I am looking forward to work again. I can hardly wait to find out what's been going on these past ten days.

Group H.Q.
R.C.A.F. Overseas
Sept. 30th, 1944

To continue about my recent Leave....I went to sleep on the train, en route to Wales from Manchester. It was due in Colwyn Bay an hour earlier than I had been told, so I slept past the station and had to taxi back, to the amusement of my relatives. It was like awaking in a dream to see mountains and the sea. A wet fortnight previously had turned everything green and very lovely.

The cousins I found entirely delightful. The family includes two boys of eighteen, John and Jack. John is waiting to go into the R.A.F. and Jack has won a scholarship to Cambridge. Goes down this month, to study engineering. Barbara, twenty-two, works in one of the Ministry Offices. She is a charming girl and I took a great shine to her. We went over to a parade of the Women's Junior Air Training Cadets the first night I was there. It confirmed me in the opinion that such things ought to be kept on after the war.

The rest of the time in Wales – Thursday and Friday – we cycled miles, and walked more miles and climbed endless hills. We visited Conway Castle, went to Llandudno, Colwyn Bay, Conway town and to the top of Bryn Euryn and the Great Orme. The scenery was marvellous. The last evening, the boys took Barbara and me to a dance at the Winter Gardens.

They dance well – the two lads – better than the average. As someone said, "Englishmen dance with you as though they weren't there". A large sign said "Jitterbugging forbidden until 10 p.m." At ten the Yanks took over the floor and put on a show! The only other Canadians present, two sodden Flying Officers based in Northern Ireland, came over and were very amusing. One of them turned to me and said, "Madam, may I borrow your frame for this struggle?" I had almost forgotten the old Canadian line! The English cousins were highly amused.

It was the next day in London that I heard about Chris. Piece by piece we did learn that it wasn't serious. Have had two letters from him since. It's definitely a "Blighty" and may put him out of the war for good. Shrapnel went right through his shin.

The rest of my leave went quickly and when I got back to camp they said, "You're going to Group H.Q. Ha-ha". Ha-ha! It's not funny; however I'll be among old friends such as Mona. Being "joed" to work at H.Q. is something I have never aspired to. But I'd have bartered my soul for this posting two months ago. Have been supremely happy at my present Station.

----

6 Group H.Q.
RCAF Overseas
Oct. 5th, 1944

The new posting came while I was on Leave. They were kind enough not to recall me – though they'd have had to catch me first! There's only one thing that takes longer than clearing from a Station, and that's getting signed on to the new one. As I see it, the prime requisite to qualify for an Orderly Room Clerk is the ability to ignore people from a distance of five feet, or not to see them at all. If you're led to the Recruiting Office by a Seeing-Eye dog, then you automatically qualify as an Orderly Room Sergeant. I have concluded this while waiting endless hours for the signatures necessary before actually being "signed on" at a new post.

Am very comfortably settled. (Well, comfortable, anyway, though not exactly settled yet. That takes time!) Was lucky enough to get a bed in the same hut as Mona. There are fifteen of us together. Mostly M.T. drivers, a couple of Wireless Ops and Mona and Cherry, who are shift-workers. Plus two or three cooks. My bunk is close to the fire, which is in the middle of the hut, so it's nice and warm, if too softening for health. The crowd – many of whom I knew before – are remarkably nice girls and I feel quite at home due to their welcome.

The food is excellent. We had corn on the cob yesterday – the first I've had in England. There was apple pie, chocolate cake, stewed Damson plums, and potato chips. No, we are not doing badly. What a contrast to other Stations!

In the fall of 1944 we were lucky enough to locate some corn on the cob that was for human consumption and someone prevailed on a Sergeant in the Mess to cook it for us. At that time in Britain, no one else would have dreamed of salivating over something that was generally considered feed for cattle or pigs. But for us it was a rare and wonderful treat, and a reminder of home that kept our spirits up.

Well anyway, I'm enjoying working in the Group H.Q.'s Intelligence Office. It's certainly a paper war. Seven copies of everything is the secret of success, I see. Have a lovely new supply of coloured pencils and my very own bottle of India ink. Things are looking up.

There is a bit more spit and polish here at Group H.Q. than on a Flying station due to the prevalence of Knobs (high-ranking officers), but not much. Beds have to be stacked once a week. [*The term "stacking" meant stripping the beds, right down to the bed-springs – such as they were – and folding the sheets and covers. For Inspection, the three pieces of the mattress were "stacked", with the folded blankets on top and next the sheets. Finally, the bolster or pillow and pillowcase were neatly set in place. It was tiresome to have to do this and often, later, when we returned to re-make our beds, there was every possibility that everything would be damp as well as cold.*] There are practically no parades. We had a Church Parade on Sunday, by the way. It was Harvest Festival. The Station Commander marched us down to the village church and the Padre took the Service.

The days are shortening remarkably quickly and winter is closing in. The month of September was, on the whole, beautiful. London was green and lovely in the spring, but no lovelier than on those fine September days. It's frosty now, night and morning, but still warm at noon. The view from the Castle across a tiny lake to the rugged Yorkshire countryside – hills, forest and moors – is reminiscent of Algonquin Park, even to the coniferous trees.

The Castle has been well-looked after. Temporary partitions have been put up inside, and wooden stairs protect the wide staircase. It must have been quite a place in peace time. They say there's a ghost, but unless I work at night – which is unlikely – I'll miss seeing it (him/her?) My working hours are 8:30-5:30 with a day off a week and it's unusual to have ghosts on the day-shift, I think.

The epic of Arnhem is history now. It was one of the major subjects of conversation at the time. The lifting (partial) of the black-out also loomed large in our lives. If we, who have been subject to black-outs for only ten months, were delighted, you can imagine what it meant to the people who have had it for five years.

Having barely settled into the routine and workings of Group HQ in Knaresborough, I found myself back at my previous posting at #62 Base, Linton. The rationale behind these apparently random moves escaped me at the time, but I was perfectly happy to be "returned to sender". I later discovered it had all been due to a clerical error and when it came to light I was dispatched back to Linton in short order.

On my return I was informed that I would again be sharing the duties of Map Clerk with a WAAF Corporal. It was our job to keep the inventory of the maps that the crews would need on their flights. The maps were stored flat, in immense map drawers. After each trip we cleaned up the maps returned to us by the Navigators, prior to re-filing them. There would be pencilled marks and navigational estimates to be removed.

Once we'd been informed of the target for an impending trip, we would check which maps a crew would need. It might require four maps to get an aircraft to its target and home again. We would extract four dozen maps, if there were twelve crews going out, and fold each map, before delivering them to the adjacent Briefing Room. If the planes were diverted by bad weather on their return flight and had to land at some other Station, we might not get our maps back until the crews touched down a day or so later, but normally we would collect our maps as the Boys went in to de-briefing.

When the planes returned from an Operation, the Station was far from asleep. Ground Crews were waiting anxiously – each crew on alert for its own aircraft. The kitchen staff, meanwhile, was preparing to serve up the eggs that the aircrew were entitled to after a raid. The Control Tower was busy listening for the sound of the first returnees and issuing orders to the pilots once radio contact had been established. A WD Sergeant would then mark the time of arrival of each crew up on a board – the time of take-off and the names of the crew having already been recorded beside each pilot-captain's name. Another WD was receiving reports from our two satellite Stations over a radio-transmitter or a scrambled telephone line concerning their returning crews and their successes over the Target. Headquarters for our Group was Knaresborough, Yorkshire and in turn, it received totals of planes returned, diverted or still missing.

The cold, tired crews would filter in, pick up a mug of hot tea laced with rum, and then be de-briefed by the Intelligence people as quickly as possible. The Met (meteorological) Officer and the Padre were always among those who hovered, as we all watched and waited for the blank spaces on the blackboard to be filled in.

Sgt. Zella (Stade) Clarke marking the Operations Board at #62 Base, Linton-on-Ouse, Yorkshire.

Collection of Mrs. W.V. Beaulieu, UK 16242

I don't know what the big idea was (moving to HQ and back again), but I was sorry to leave Mona and the gang and yet am glad to be back here with Paddy and Co. I am once again in my old niche; this time working on maps and charts. Hope I've settled down this time.

Today is very reminiscent of the weather at home at this time of year. It lacks the colour, however. I would say autumn is definitely *the* season in England.

Each departure from a Station has called for a celebration of sorts, and last night my return to the fold at Base meant that Paddy and several others and I went into York. The actor Nigel Bruce's brother, Sir Michael, a F/L Intelligence, was very much part of the party, – and added greatly to it. He has tales of every imaginable escapade in almost

Sgts. Margot Norum (left) and Bev Lye (right) at the walls of the city of York, 1944.
Collection of Mrs. W.V. Beaulieu

every country. At the same time, the Wing Commander of one of our Squadrons was entertaining his brother and a number of other Canadian Army types who are over here on a Cook's Tour. The drive back to camp was in the nature of a low-level bombing attack, but we arrived all right, which is the main thing.

The scene: Sitting in front of Paddy's fire in the living-room of the Sergeants' house. The characters: Paddy, Bev, and I. The operations: quaffing cocoa and eating toast and jam. It's a howling night – one of those Yorkshire gales – and here are we, snug as we can be!

We've been quite busy. And when the weather isn't so good, there's always the question of whether their fuel will hold out until the boys get all the way back. So the element of suspense is never lacking.

The initiation of a new kite is one of our chief excitements. The plane arrives without a name, to replace some veteran that has "gone for a Burton". She is taken on her maiden trip by any crew whose plane is unserviceable at the time. They may take her a couple of times before their own is ready for business again. Then she fills in when needed until a new crew arrives ready for their Ops. By then "S for Sugar" or "B for Bobbie" has begun to develop a personality all her own, and before you know it, her crew won't fly in anything else. Each ground crew takes a special pride in servicing, refitting and refuelling its own kite for its own air-crew and its Operations are the most keenly followed.

Each section of the camp is competing to buy the largest number of Victory Bonds. The total objective is eighty thousand dollars.

62 Base
R.C.A.F.
Oct. 23rd, 1944

We've sort of lost track of old George lately. No address for him since the 13th. I had a letter from him yesterday dated the 9th, saying he was taking over the Company and would be too busy to write for awhile; but that his faith was as strong as ever. It will probably be some time before details come through, so we'll just have to wait and see.

Nov. 3rd, 1944

There isn't really any news – or if there is, it escapes me. Our own private Underground is working tooth and nail to unearth info pertinent to the disappearance of one husband, slightly used.

Three months seems no time at all to you and me, but in that time the Unit has seen many come and go, and there are few left who were with the 1st Battalion in brighter Brighton days. The same is true of *all* the Canadian Regiments over there. You might be glad to hear that the Canadian Army is regarded here as a sort of super-Commando outfit. If anyone ever doubted that the troops were not wasting their time during their four-year wait in England, those doubts have vanished. The people who, up till June, were just a trifle leery of the Friendly Invasion of troops who were eating the country's food and burning the country's fuel, have eaten their words in the face of what the boys are doing in Europe.

Yes, I repeat... Fall here is the best. Today is lovely – clear and sunny – with not a hint of what Winter has in store for us. These are the warm days and cool nights, with darkness closing in increasingly early and mists settling over the moors with the going down of the sun. The full moon and these same mists combine to make an eerie, not-of-this-earth sensation, reminiscent of *The Hounds of the Baskervilles*... All we need are a few wolves – and perhaps we have those!

Mon., 13th Nov., 1944.

I was expecting Derrick Farmiloe, an RAF friend from Digby, for a little revelry in York on the 20th of October. Half an hour before I left to go into town to meet him, I went to collect my mail. There was only a yellow envelope and I thought, "Damn – it's Derrick. He can't come." Instead, of course, it was " Regret to inform you ... Missing in Action, October thirteenth."

I had a letter this week from Col. Ritchie (Black Watch Regiment) written on Oct. 16th. The Colonel confirmed what I had already been hearing. There was a sticky attack and then a hopeless situation. From posts of observation, they watched the group George was with being marched off, and subsequently the enemy came back and collected the wounded. They think George was among the latter group. He left his cap behind.

I had long thought that word that someone was "Missing" was extremely bad news, but when I received the wire about George, I found that it provided a degree of comfort. At least he hadn't been killed! I telephoned his Aunt Olga Buch at the Daily Express to let her know, and also Grant Hollingworth, the Padre at No. 1 Canadian Neurological Hospital at Basingstoke, where I'd visited on several occasions. Within minutes I had Grant's report from some patients – Black Watch men – who had been in the same battle on the Schelde on Black Friday, October 13, 1944 and had seen George being taken off by German stretcher-bearers. They had heard him call out, " Don't take my cap. I'll be back for it."

My immediate thought was that I should cable his family and also mine to inform them that according to my sources it appeared that George was all right and that I hoped we'd be celebrating March 8 (my birthday) together. Back came the cables from the censors. Who was "George"? Why was he "all right"? What was the significance of March 8th? And so on. As a result the cables were delayed by a week.

Meanwhile George's Aunt Olga, with access to the Daily Express wire service, had cabled both our families saying "Deepest Sympathy", and in the process left all concerned totally in the dark. There was no indication in the cable whether it referred to George, my brother, Chris, or even (though less likely) myself. Within a few days, my father, through his Army connections, was able to have a look at a casualty list and confirm that George was among the twenty-four men from the Black Watch Regiment listed as Missing on October 13. Later on, official word came through that George was a Prisoner of War in northern Germany; however it was the New Year before we actually heard from him.

We had an Air Vice-Marshal's Parade this week, which is one of the horrors of war. Thank God they are few and far between – these parades. We stood waiting for His Nibs for two hours in a hangar and it seemed like twelve. When he finally arrived, he forgot to stand us at ease. It took him and the other Brass Hats half an hour to felicitate each other over the P.A. system and to tell each other how nice it was to be there and then to present a Coat of Arms to 62 Base. Our feet were glued to the spot, when it was all over. All I could think of was the amount of work waiting to be done.

Nov. 17th, 1944

Winter is setting in. Every morning I grumble about getting up in the dark. It's a change, at least, from grumbling about plain ordinary rising in the summer,

S/L Bruce "Bud" Brittain, DFC. A former classmate at Macdonald College in Ste. Anne de Bellevue, Quebec.

Collection of W. B. Brittain

though. However, I now am well-clad in "Baffle Dress", as I think I may have told you and certainly our billets are comparatively cosy, so we think we're pretty lucky.

They talk of sending the married gals home soon, and I s'pose that's better than staying here and being stranded while George gets home first!

More details about George filter through, bit by bit. People certainly have been good about writing what they hear, and it all adds up to the same thing. It seems likely that he was not long without medical attention and he is thought to have been not seriously hurt. He left his Balmoral on the Field and one of the patients in Grant Hollingworth's hospital, who was there, has been wearing his Hackle (*a red feather worn in the Balmoral as a battle honour*) ever since. I can't but think that the cap being left behind was no accident.

Dec. 4th, 1944

Guess who knocked on the door and came in yesterday – Bud Brittain! [*Bruce "Bud" Brittain had been a classmate of mine in the School for Teachers and was the son of Col. William Brittain of Macdonald College in Ste. Anne de Bellevue, who'd travelled with me on the same train when I was en route to Ottawa for Basic Training almost two years earlier.*] I could have hugged him, I was so pleased to see him. He's still the same old Bud – a little taller perhaps, and a little broader, but same old grin – and the same old laugh. I wasn't busy at the time, so he sat down by the fire and we had a chat. He and his crew came down to get a kite, and should have taken off at eleven a.m., but a cold front loomed up, so in popped Bud again in the afternoon.

Once it had been established that George was being held at Oflag 79, a great deal of trans-Atlantic correspondence ensued about the sending of parcels to a POW. Technically only his next-of-kin was entitled to send a parcel, however my mother felt that a parcel should be sent out from Canada, since food and clothing were more readily available there. George's parents, living in New York, had the same idea and both families thought I should transfer my next-of-kin status to them.

In the end, it was agreed that my mother and mother-in-law would put together a parcel in Montreal; however, because of the chaos of those final months of the war in Europe, George did not receive any parcels from home nor, for that matter, any mail of any description. When Oflag 79 was liberated by General Patton's G.I.'s in mid-April 1945, it seems that great stock-piles of food – and possibly parcels – were found sitting at the gate of the camp, but by then the matter of parcels and mail meant far less than it would have in the preceding months.

This flurry of correspondence over the parcel situation, in addition to my own duties and the reality that the end of the war seemed imminent, meant that my letters to Marion Strang and others became more infrequent during the last few months of my overseas service. I also knew nothing of the fact that each of my letters to Mrs. Strang was being carefully set aside in anticipation of my safe return to Canada.

December 31st, 1944.

I had a letter today from George written on October 25th. He said he had taken cover after being hit and had been spotted by the German Red Cross. German paratroopers had picked him up and were very decent. He has a hole in his right thigh (probably shrapnel) and a slashed wrist, but no bones broken and George says that in the course of time his leg will be all right. The only personal possessions he has are a tunic and a sweater – and his purse with my picture in it. He adds that the medical attention is good. Could my New Year's Eve have been better?

Christmas was rather a shambles here – foggy both inside and out. Dinner was good and the place was awash with beer. I stayed strictly sober and tried to enjoy kissing all the boys. Now that the fog has lifted, we are working hard. I've been on duty all day and most of the night for the last three days and am thoroughly exhausted. I was detailed for a Church Parade in York today, to celebrate the second anniversary of the Canadian Bomber Group. Frozen to the marrow, I slept through the service, so I can't recount much of it.

Did I tell you the latest quip about why the Zombies are like V-2's ? Because we don't know when *they're* coming over, either!

Those men who had been enlisted for military service in Canada only – as opposed to volunteering for overseas duty – quickly came to be referred to as Zombies, and were the target of many jokes and snide remarks among Service people and civilians alike.

Essentially, the politics of conscription was not of much interest to most of us women in the Services. We had volunteered, and knew we could be sent anywhere, and that was all there was to it. The men whom we knew on Active Service were too busy, on the whole, to be very concerned about the whole issue, either. In any case, it wasn't a topic of discussion when we got together, unless it was to pass on the latest Zombie joke.

Our C.O., Group Captain Claire Annis, has been posted away – unhappily for us. Someone said today that it would have been worthwhile joining the RCAF just to know him and that's about the size of it. He is universally liked. He made it a practice to give us as much time off as he could when there was no flying and expected one hundred per cent effort when we were busy – and he got it. The boys would do anything he asked.

There isn't much discipline on a Flying Station in the RCAF. And the boys knew that if they had to work all day and all night for two or three days at a time, the Groupie would make it up to them somehow. He always did, too. We've always had the feeling that we were being taken into his confidence. He'd "tannoy" a message over the loud speaker system just before a specially big Operation, telling us as much as he could of the situation and afterwards he'd thank the Station. That kind of morale doesn't come wrapped with the meat.

Jan. 17th, 1945

Somehow we are getting through all this. My saintly Corporal has taken an extra week's sick leave, leaving the bag in my tender and well-meaning care. I have been told that, since I am no longer singing "Come Out, Come Out, Wherever You Are" to George, this puts me in the group who have had it, and should be wending their way homewards.

The Flight Officer says that there is a chance that I may be proved irreplaceable since I am now the *only* WD Map Clerk in the U.K.! – the other one having fallen by the way-side. (The same Flt/O admits that I am a unique specimen, as she heaves a sigh of relief that I am not twins!) There may yet be an advantage to being a Square Peg! Anyway, it will all come out in the wash, and I have reprieve for yet another few days (weeks?... months?...)

A Trade Board Exam looms up next week and I have been attempting to prepare for it in a hit-and-miss manner in odd spare moments. It shouldn't be as hard as some others I've squeezed through, and I am not unduly worried about it.

The RCAF had no Trade known as Map Clerk, so as a Clerk Op I was performing a Map Clerk's duties. This caused a degree of consternation, since it involved the level of pay – including Trades Pay – and was considered altogether highly irregular. Eventually, though, the RCAF came up with a solution. London HQ sent a letter to every Station in the U.K which had any RCAF personnel, stating that the Trade of Map Clerk had been officially opened. Before anyone could draw breath, a second letter was fired off to the effect that the Trade had been closed, since the quota for

*Map Clerks was now filled. (The quota consisting of one – Leading
Airwoman Buch.)*

*This appeared to have settled the matter until I returned to Canada
later that same year and was about to be demobilized. Of necessity the issue
of my designation as a Map Clerk resurfaced. How could a WD declaring
that she was a Map Clerk possibly be discharged when – according to the
RCAF- no such Trade existed? So the procedure had to be reversed and I
reverted to my original classification as Clerk Ops. This, of course, entailed
the re- writing of the Clerk Ops exams on the spot, in order that my Trade
level be officially established. Above all, conformity must prevail.*

One of the other girls cleaned up the cupboards tonight and threw a lot of stuff
into the fire – including a cartridge – which of course exploded. (They do,
sometimes!) I had only time to talk to St. Peter for a minute before we found
out we weren't at all dead. (St. Peter was skeptical about letting me in. Said I
asked too many questions. All I wanted to know was whether they had any coal
there...) We have had a few nasty accidents with bombed-up aircraft exploding
recently – these latter, incidentally, seem so much worse than losses to the
enemy.

Was lucky enough to be able to see the D'Oyly Carte Company's
presentation of *Patience* last week and enjoyed it. Went to the Sunday evening
Record Hour in the "Y" lounge and also saw *Stormy Weather* – a film of ancient
vintage with an all-negro cast, including Cab Calloway.

Feb. 6th, 1945

I've been told that I'd be home in plenty of time to plant my Easter Eggs. The
ensuing turmoil didn't make for letter-writing. Our Flt/O has just left. We had
a party for her last night. Half the girls are complaining because they *want* to go
home – the other half because they *are!* Is there anything quite as extraordinary
as the female mind? I think not!

Anyway, one-twelfth of a dozen WAAFs are being ordered to take my place.
There will be a short period of double-banking – a fortnight or so – and then
"I've 'ad it". Anything from a month (or three weeks) to about six weeks and it's
life on the ocean wave. Even at that, had it not been for someone's
consideration in giving me more time, I'd be going sooner. So one does have to
count oneself lucky, I guess.

The only thing that has prevented post-leave doldrums is the amount of
work – plus intermittent excitement. You've never seen me when my hair stood
straight up on end from sheer fright, have you? It's rather a sight, I should
think. First command: "To the shelters". First thought: "God, they're full of
water". – Second command: "As you were. Take cover!"

There is talk of restoring the black-out – which seems a pity, when the evenings are just beginning to be light and people feel like stirring from the fireside. It's *Spring!* The crocuses are up and we are discarding our greatcoats.

The blackout had been partially lifted in rural areas which were away from London and the mechanical buzz-bombs. Germany was using these to attack London and environs in a last-ditch effort to destroy and demoralize the British.

March 5th, 1945

Was interested to find, when I got back from Leave, that home postings have been frozen for the time being, so here we go again. No Easter Eggs planted, I can see. What a life!

Upon my return I found a letter from some people in Northumberland, whose son has just come back on a hospital ship from Germany, badly hurt. He brought with him a note from George, written Dec. 6th. George was most depressed, but saying that he was O.K. and near Brunswick at that time. The lad who brought the note had lost both hands and an eye and his parents said that George had been able to help in some way. Poor youngster! And yet his parents' letter was so full of joy at having him back at all. It breaks your heart!

We have a mechanical cow here now. It beats up whole (powdered)

Lt. Chris Hawkins recuperating in Hereford, England, 1945.

milk and refrigerates it, so that it tastes like the "Real Thing". You may think of me doing a little Black Marketing on the side, such as trading my chocolate ration for an extra drink. It's a remarkably fine contraption, our Betsy! No one has to feed her, either. We have been talking about tampering with the refrigerator so that the milk would *freeze.* Ice cream daily, if so...

When the RCAF, WD Messing Officers in Ottawa wanted to let their counterparts in England know that this splendid machine was being shipped overseas, they sent a cable saying "Greetings from the Udder Side". The censors must have been left puzzling over that particular communique for some time!

Airwoman Mary Buch, Linton-on-Ouse, Yorkshire, 1945.

It continues to be warm and gloriously sunny, and we wish we could take the roof off and work in the sunshine. It's still cold indoors, making a fire a necessity.

Mona has been given her ticket and I shall be saying au revoir to her tomorrow. I thought mine would be along, too, but a complete right-about-face in H.Q.'s policy says that P.O.W.'s wives are now to be treated as *single* and we are to stay. I had just written to Queen's to inquire about summer courses and was telling myself that a little Latin would be a good thing – also some Economics. Guess it' ll be *next* summer!

George is at Oflag 79 now, near Brunswick. He has met many Montrealers, including some lads from the Regiment, two of whom are old school pals from B.C.S. [*Bishops's College School in Lennoxville, P.Q.*] and one of whom is from Lukis-Stewart, his office. Beside one lad's name he wrote in brackets, "Dorchester Hotel Elevator". I thought he meant the lad worked there, until I remembered that George, Mona and I had met him the night before our marriage, in the midst of a blitz, in an elevator! There are reunions in the strangest places.

The mechanical cow is giving us milk every day now. And would you believe it, last week – cream of mushroom soup. Pretty good animal to be able to do that. I wonder what they feed her. Petrol, I guess.

While awaiting news of George's release, I was able to spend time with my brother, Chris, who had returned from hospital in France and was gradually getting back on his feet again. He had been wounded in

September. *After surgery in France and again in England for the removal of shrapnel, he was sent to Garnon's in Herefordshire to recuperate. Garnon's was the stately home of Vincent Massey, Canada's High Commissioner to the U.K., which he and his wife, Alice, had generously given over for use as a convalescent hospital for Canadian officers.*

I was able to visit Chris there, while on Leave, and stayed in Hereford at a local inn for an enjoyable three days. We visited the cathedral, and also remarked on the vast herds of sheep, the red cattle and the half-timbered houses. The region's apple cider also played its part in our happy reunion and there was much talk of Home and family and people we both knew. By the time he was well enough to go back on Active Service, the war was almost over, so Chris remained in England as an Education Officer working with repatriated troops as they began to appear. This was an essential but long-term position, and it was January 1946 before he was finally able to return home.

18th March, 1945

While on Leave in London, Chris and I walked down Piccadilly to Regent's Square, where we deliberated upon the choice of a "flick". We finally went to *Arsenic and Old Lace*. I haven't seen the play, but if the film is any indication, it must be riotous. Chris and I both enjoyed it immensely.

I came back to camp on the morning train. The trains are crowded now. Spring and fine weather take everyone on Leave to the south and as well, there are all the rotation boys from the Front who are lucky enough to win in the draw. The hotels and the streets; the shops and the movies are all crowded with happy throngs, too – with a very *large* hint of Victory in the air!

We get into the groove of Operations and nothing matters but getting the kites off and having them come back and hearing that they pranged the target in the approved manner. It has been a terrific month to date and all sorts of records are being broken. Into the bargain we've had a few upsetting accidents and, if away from it for a day or longer, we always come back feeling like caged animals. It's silly, because there's no place at this moment that we'd rather be!

I expected to have another exam in Maps next month, in order to regain the "props" and the L.A.W. (Leading Air Woman) I thought I'd lost in the remuster from one trade to another. It turns out that they gave me my props back on the strength of what I did in January's exam. It was embarrassingly easy, but that's not the way I'll tell it, of course. We're wearing our tin hats now and then – just to make sure they fit. I, for one, don't care if I never see one again. What it must be like after five and a half years, I can't imagine.

March 23rd, 1945

The weather has been pleasant. Perfection, in fact. We cycled out to the perimeter track yesterday, to watch take-off. Something I never tire of – no matter how often.

Oranges are in the canteen now, and we are getting eggs from the local farmers in quantity. These and the daily quota of milk encourage us in the belief that we are living like kings.

Sunday, 25th March, 1945

Have spent the morning riding around the perimeter track helping to clear up debris from a kite that crashed on take-off, so that the boys will have a clear deck to land on. Nuts, bolts, shrapnel, bullets are all that remain after the fire.

The jamboree at which Dr. James (the Principal of McGill) spoke last night was a success. About thirty of us from here went. There were at least three hundred present from the RCAF Stations in the vicinity. It was a remarkably good program and Dr. James' talk was very apropos. I am not sure that most of us here have not a distorted view of some of Canada's problems, both present and post-war. But they seem less remote after hearing James. He could have made it all seem so easy – this business of conversion from war to peace – but he didn't and he went over in a big way.

There was a hectic question period afterwards. Group Captain Lowe also spoke. He's stationed at Ottawa as chief of the education section of the RCAF. (In peace-time, he was Director of Education in Manitoba.) James told us what we wanted to know and it is a source of satisfaction to us to hear what is being planned at home. It ought also to be an encouragement to James and others to see that the Services really are doing some thinking about education and the future.

Afterwards I had a very brief chat with Dr. James. I had heard nothing of Bud Brittain and had been wondering whether he had finished his tour, since his name hasn't appeared in the crew-lists lately. Dr. James said "Missing" and if this is so, then there is – as always – much to hope for. I shall inquire from someone on Bud's Station to find out what they know. Bud was known to be a good pilot and he was being primed for more responsibility. Dr. Brittain's illness will add further anxiety to the family. It is a trying time for them all and I am sorry. I hope cheering news of Bud reaches his people soon. About Bud himself I find myself unable to say anything. [*Happily, Bud turned up at the end of the war, after being shot down off the west coast of Denmark on his way home from laying mines in Rostock harbour. Both his gunners were killed but he was hauled out of the water and hospitalized by the occupation forces in Denmark. He was subsequently transferred to a POW camp in Germany and was later liberated by American troops.*]

It has been a chapter of accidents here lately. It never rains but it pours. Everyone is feeling very, very tired. It's not the healthy fatigue of effort, but the weariness of consistent application of nerve and sinew.

News that another crossing of the Rhine has been made has acted as a stimulus and the boys have perked up considerably. There is certainly no equal division of labour and those of us whose lot it is to work moderate hours in a fairly even routine can only wish that we could relieve the boys from flying. (It's probably a very good thing that we can't! "Butcher" Harris, head of Bomber Command, has enough troubles and worries, without the added one of WDs taking off in his precious aircraft! I can almost see his face!)

Much as some of us would have loved the chance to get airborne, the time for women at the controls had not yet arrived. Flying aside, throughout the duration of this tour of overseas duty, it was collectively assumed that if something needed to be done, whoever happened to be close at hand would see to it. If a bomber crashed on landing or take-off, all available personnel immediately rushed to get the runway clear. There was no muttering about seniority, overtime, job classifications or discrimination. Any officer or Other Rank who was not otherwise engaged would simply pick up a broom and set to work.

There were, of course, other less dramatic tasks; but these, too, were accomplished with dispatch. A sudden snowfall? A waste-basket to be dumped? Some leftover filing from a previous shift that had been especially busy? Anything that needed doing simply got done. And heaven help anyone inclined to attempt avoidance tactics. Potential slackers were soon set straight in no uncertain terms. In post-war days, this positive attitude of pulling together tended to carry over into the workplace, once everyone had returned safely to hearth and home.

April 2nd, 1945

Things are moving at the Front and our work is almost a thing of the past now. Seems strange to think that we are actually slackening off, with V-E Day not yet here. There is plenty of routine-work, but very little of the other.

April 11th, 1945

We are in the throes of preparing for a visit from a Very Important Person (Guesses are cheap and mine is Princess Mary) so there are limits on that much talked-of "free time". Parade every morning at eight and no excuses accepted. Can think of things I'd rather do. The advantage is that at least we're awake now when we get to work!

The Hun isn't the only one getting licked. The Jap seems to be getting his too. The pieces of the puzzle are fitting together and it will finally spell complete victory, but what chaos the world is in!

In December 1944, a plane from one of our Squadrons shot down a single-engine German fighter and it was discovered that the enemy had begun using jet-propelled aircraft. On April 25th, 1945, our two Squadrons at Linton – 426 (Thunderbird) and 408 (Goose) – went out on what was to be their final bombing operation over Wangerooge Island, east of the Fresian Chain. We lost one crew, and because we sensed that the end of the war in Europe was imminent, the loss of these young lives seemed all the more poignant.

April 18th, 1945

Official word that George is liberated and on his way back here comes also with the news that Bud Brittain is all right. I think of how little hope was held here for Bud's safety and I marvel at the miracle. One of our Wing Commanders tells me that Bud is in a hospital with a broken leg. I am rather keen to hear what happened but no one here knows yet. Numbers of our crews, who have been reported as Missing, have turned up in the last ten days or so. It 's encouraging.

Parades go on as usual. We have been surprisingly busy suddenly, as well. The weather is breaking all records and it's really *hot* in the sun. We planted some vegetable seeds in our back garden and we're beginning to wonder what will come up. It looks as though we might have to start watering, if it doesn't rain.

Tues. April 24th, 1945

This was the day of the visit of the Princess Royal. Things went very well indeed. We had our usual eight o'clock Parade yesterday and another in the afternoon which lasted an hour and a half. The sun was in our eyes by then and we were late for our tea, so we were not happy!

This morning dawned fair and cool, though, and we were all in our places by ten-fifteen. The Senior Officers arrived at ten-thirty and at a quarter to eleven – as scheduled – the Princess's car drove up. As soon as she had been met by the C.O., the band played "God Save the King" for the Royal Salute. Next followed the Inspection and then the March Past. We retired to our Sections after the Parade.

A few of us were posted to the Flying Control Tower and after her visit there, we were presented to H.R.H. She was wearing the uniform of the Auxiliary Territorial Service – khaki, with much red on cap and lapels. The Princess is very like the pictures of her mother, and Princess Elizabeth resembles

Mary and George Buch on his return to England after his liberation from Oflag 79
in Germany, April 1945.

her a lot. She asked the usual questions about our length of service, and whether we were happy here.

As we were presented, our officer gave her a clue about each of us. It seems her own son has been a P.O.W. and was moved when our Armies advanced, so she doesn't know where he is now. Paddy called her "Your Majesty" by mistake, which amused her. Apart from that and the fact that the Group-Captain asked me on Parade, as they inspected, why the Truant Officer hadn't caught up with me, it was all terribly serious! (The G.C. has a bit of mischief about him, and it would come out at a time like that!)

The hectic rehearsals for all this and the frantic polishing up in the office for the occasion, have left us all rather done-in. Mac and I went to see Somerset Maugham's *The Breadwinner* last night, which was put on by the York Rep and was well done.

Within two weeks, the long awaited surrender of Nazi Germany followed close on the heels of George's repatriation to England. Once Oflag 79 had been liberated, it was only a matter of days before the POWs were flown back to England to be checked out at Army Hospitals. On George's release, I was given Leave and we spent the first few days in a flat lent to us by friends in Park Lane. The official declaration of Victory was expected any day and the atmosphere in London was one of incomparable jubilation.

In the interests of George's recuperation, we decided to journey down to Shanklin on the Isle of Wight. The little hotel we stayed at was bursting at the seams with officers and their wives, and it was there that we heard Churchill's famous broadcast announcing that May 8, 1945 would officially be declared V-E Day – Victory in Europe after six long years.

May 7th, 1945
V–E Day!!

George and I are sitting in the lounge of a little hotel in Shanklin on the Isle of Wight awaiting Churchill's speech which is due in half an hour. All the toasts today are to Victory in the East and you are very much in my thoughts. May the Victory soon be complete!

While we were in Waterloo Station the other day, along came Bud Brittain, looking like a millionaire. He still has a cast on his foot. He is at the same hospital where Chris was when I visited him in March and had just had a "48" to go back to visit the Squadron. He, too, will be home soon with adventures to tell you!

George is well, though he has lost a lot of weight. It becomes him, but he is lacking in strength. The treatment of the boys has not been brutal, but they were starved for some time. At the moment George is on double rations with an added quart of milk and all the Stout he can drink. He is walking miles daily and already looks a hundred per cent better.

One of the big events last week was a party at the Dorchester, given by the Allied Services Officers' Welcoming Committee. I have never seen such an array of Allied uniforms – The Princess Royal, Lord Wavell and Lady Louis Mountbatten were guests of honour and there were people from all over the Empire as well as Holland, France, Russia, Belgium and so on. We met some of George's "ex-kriegie" friends, as they call themselves, and had dinner together.

From Shanklin we headed north to Glasgow; however, getting through London on V-E Day proved to be a somewhat daunting exercise. The streets were thronging with people and transportation was catch-as-catch-can. Rationing of liquor and food was abandoned as people waved flags and hugged each other, sang and danced, laughed and cried, then laughed again.

From Glasgow we travelled on to Edinburgh and as luck would have it, that same night Edinburgh Castle was flood-lit for the first time since 1939. To us this glorious sight symbolized the true end of the war in Europe and we set our sights on Home.

After our four week's Leave, I returned to Linton. By this time, the end of May had come and gone. George and I had one more meeting in London for a weekend before he sailed for Canada in mid-June. During the few days we were together in London, I was feeling a little off-colour and George and I made our way to RCAF Medical H.Q. to determine whether or not I was pregnant. In their wisdom, the doctors decided this was not the case and George and I parted in hopes that I, too, would soon be homeward bound.

Torquay
R.C.A.F. "R" Depot,
June 18th, 1945

Here we are on the last leg of our trip. George went last week, and must be home by now. Things are uncertain at the moment but with luck another ten days or two weeks will see us en route. Meanwhile, Torquay is providing everything that could be desired. We are billeted in a hotel overlooking the sea, and June is the month to be here. Thanks to the sunshine, we are all beginning to look a little less as though we had just crawled out from under a rock. Last night two of us took a bus out to Babbacombe, about five or six miles from Torquay, and walked back across the Downs.

This is a part of the England I had read about. It really exists! We scrambled down paths to the beaches and climbed steep ascents to look out across sand and cliffs to the ocean. Tor Bay is bluer than anything I have ever seen. I could only wonder that once I had considered mere words adequate. The honeysuckle is in bloom and every rose-bush is a mass of blossom. The gardens are ablaze, and the foliage here is a rare combination of palms and pines. The little boys on the beaches are learning to fly their first kites, no longer prohibited by security regulations. It would not be surprising if people got Torquay confused with the Promised Land!

The season is much earlier here, of course, than in the north of England, so we are excited by fresh vegetables. We have all the tomatoes and lettuce we can eat. The food in our Mess is excellent.

At last we have been able to turn in our gas equipment and tin hats, which has lightened our load considerably. I shed not a tear as I parted with my respirator!

Am off to the Knights of Columbus Canteen now. We can buy Cokes, Canadian chocolate bars and chicken sandwiches there. All This and Heaven Too!

One never knows. I might decide to settle here, although I must admit that Canada looks pretty good, at this point..!

During my stay at the depot in Torquay, awaiting orders to be shipped home, a friend who was a WD officer told me that there had been occasional miscarriages on board ship and as a result there had been an equal number of very unhappy husbands. The solution, it seems, was that once pregnancy was definitely confirmed, the Servicewoman in question would not be permitted to travel during the first trimester. Her observation was, "Once you've missed your draft home, Heaven knows when you'll get another, so it's easier if we just say you're not pregnant."

June 25, 1945

Well, one of us is home, at least... and at last! Cable from George today. And here we are in Torquay, Devon with no sign of a boat! Interest is provided in the form of my medical sheet. With that smile reserved by male M.O.'s for women who think that Nature has achieved the Supreme, the RCAF Quack says there is no little piglet on the way. Which in itself would be proof enough to me that there is!

I would prefer to think that the tests were taken too early, but fear instead that – knowing the Air Force – things have become a bit mixed up and some poor Airman has had it broken to him gently that he may be expecting... Still, if the Service says you're not going to have a baby... you're not! (King's Regulations, Air) There's no urgency about it anyway, so I'll just see the family doc when I get home. By then, he won't need a Ouija Board or a crystal ball, either!

We leave tomorrow night at midnight for Glasgow which is a twenty-four hour journey none of us is particularly looking forward to – except as a means to an end.

We've been leading a pretty lazy life, without much work. A daily Parade and a few Fatigues are all that have been asked of us. We're mighty lucky to have had three weeks here and right in the Season, too. People on vacation from London are paying several guineas a day for the same privilege we have of a holiday at Torquay!

The weather has been overcast, cloudy and dull. Today it's beautiful. I hope it lasts.

To sail homeward, in summer weather, with no blackout of the ship and no life-boat drills, was an incomparable contrast to our voyage overseas in November 1943. Toward the end of our crossing, at the point where we knew land would be sighted at any time, anticipation on board was running high. All kinds of bets were being made about the exact hour and minute that we would catch a glimpse of the distant Canadian shores.

When the great moment finally arrived, a hush came over the ship as a moment of silent gratitude was observed. This was followed by a prolonged and deafening chorus of cheers. Tears of joy welled up on all sides as the floodgates opened wide. After we had docked in Halifax and boarded the troop train bound for Montreal, "the green arms of the hills of Canada encompassed us." It was a raucous and sleepless journey. But who needed sleep? We were HOME!

On arrival, I was given a month's Leave and headed off to visit my doctor, who concurred that, as suspected, I was indeed an expectant mother and that I should return to see him again in four weeks. Then, in Rockcliffe, where I was to be discharged, this created a new cause for consternation. Not only did this Airwoman claim to be a Map Clerk when everyone knew there was no such Trade in the RCAF; but she was also claiming to be expecting a baby when the Air Force documents declared the contrary. In the end I had to cancel my doctor's appointment in Montreal until things got sorted out and all in good time our son, now fifty years old, came into the world – regulations notwithstanding!

POST SCRIPT

In retrospect – looking back on World War II from the standpoint of having worn our country's uniform with more than a little pride – I think it can be said that the majority of us enjoyed our Service experience. Unquestionably, the size of Canada's population was a contributing factor. When war broke out, the population ranged between ten and eleven million and almost inevitably people in the Canadian Forces would encounter friends or connections wherever they were posted. At the time the saying, "There are only fifty people in Canada and the rest is done with mirrors, "could easily have applied to countless situations both at home and overseas, where Service people discovered they had a common bond or mutual acquaintances. As well, particularly in the Army, the men's units were enlisted in geographically specific regions, so that they tended to call the same part of the country "home". This, in turn, fostered loyalty to their respective regiments as well as to one another, and helped perpetuate a powerful sense of camaraderie.

Few Canadian veterans of the Second World War could say that these were truly the *best* days of their lives, but there is no question that many of their recollections are happy ones – of warm friendship, mirth and mischief in the midst of loss and grief and thoughts of home and loved ones. For those of us who served overseas, the Canada we returned to had already begun an irreversible step into the Brave New World of tomorrow. There are, however, still a few lingering imprints of these times long past, which may help to ensure that all will not be filed and forgotten

Mary Hawkins Buch – RCAF (Women's Division) 1943-1945

Printed in the USA
CPSIA information can be obtained
at www.ICGtesting.com
JSHW012033140824
68134JS00033B/3030